CATHEDRALS
AND
CASTLES

Henry
James

English Journeys

PENGUIN BOOKS

Published by the Penguin Group
Penguin Books Ltd, 80 Strand, London WC2R ORL, England
Penguin Group (USA) Inc., 375 Hudson Street, New York, New York 10014, USA
Penguin Group (Canada), 90 Eglinton Avenue East, Suite 700, Toronto, Ontario, Canada M4P 2Y3
(a division of Pearson Penguin Canada Inc.)
Penguin Ireland, 25 St Stephen's Green, Dublin 2, Ireland
(a division of Penguin Books Ltd)
Penguin Group (Australia), 250 Camberwell Road, Camberwell, Victoria 3124, Australia
(a division of Pearson Australia Group Pty Ltd)
Penguin Books India Pvt Ltd, 11 Community Centre, Panchsheel Park, New Delhi – 110 017, India
Penguin Group (NZ), 67 Apollo Drive, Rosedale, North Shore 0632, New Zealand
(a division of Pearson New Zealand Ltd)
Penguin Books (South Africa) (Pty) Ltd, 24 Sturdee Avenue, Rosebank, Johannesburg 2196, South Africa

Penguin Books Ltd, Registered Offices: 80 Strand, London WC2R ORL, England

www.penguin.com

Cathedrals and Castles taken from *English Hours*
English Hours first edition in book form published in the USA by Houghton Mifflin & Co. 1905
Published in Penguin Books 2009
1

Set by Rowland Phototypesetting Ltd, Bury St Edmunds, Suffolk
Printed in England by Clays Ltd, St Ives plc

978–0–141–19086–0

www.greenpenguin.co.uk

Contents

Chester

If the Atlantic voyage be counted, as it certainly may, even with the ocean in a fairly good humour, an emphatic zero in the sum of one's better experience, the American traveller arriving at this venerable town finds himself transported, without a sensible gradation, from the edge of the New World to the very heart of the Old. It is almost a misfortune, perhaps, that Chester lies so close to the threshold of England; for it is so rare and complete a specimen of an antique town that the later-coming wonders of its sisters in renown – of Shrewsbury, Coventry, and York – suffer a trifle by comparison, and the tourist's appetite for the picturesque just loses its finer edge. Yet the first impressions of an observant American in England – of our old friend the sentimental tourist – stir up within him such a cloud of sensibility that while the charm is still unbroken he may perhaps as well dispose mentally of the greater as of the less. I have been playing at first impressions for the second time, and have won the game against a cynical adversary. I have been strolling and restrolling along the ancient wall – so perfect in its antiquity – which locks this dense little city in its stony circle, with a certain friend who has been treating me to a bitter lament on the decay of his relish for the picturesque. 'I have turned the corner of youth,' is his ceaseless plaint; 'I suspected it, but now

I know it – now that my heart beats but once where it beat a dozen times before, and that where I found sermons in stones and pictures in meadows, delicious revelations and intimations ineffable, I find nothing but the hard, heavy prose of British civilisation.' But little by little I have grown used to my friend's sad monody, and indeed feel half indebted to it as a warning against cheap infatuations.

I defied him, at any rate, to argue sucessfully against the effect of the brave little walls of Chester. There could be no better example of that phenomenon so delightfully frequent in England – an ancient property or institution lovingly readopted and consecrated to some modern amenity. The good Cestrians may boast of their walls without a shadow of that mental reservation on grounds of modern ease which is so often the tax paid by the romantic; and I can easily imagine that, though most modern towns contrive to get on comfortably without this stony girdle, these people should have come to regard theirs as a prime necessity. For through it, surely, they may know their city more intimately than their unbuckled neighbours – survey it, feel it, rejoice in it as many times a day as they please. The civic consciousness, sunning itself thus on the city's rim and glancing at the little swarming towered and gabled town within, and then at the blue undulations of the near Welsh border, may easily deepen to delicious complacency. The wall enfolds the place in a continuous ring, which, passing through innumerable picturesque vicissitudes, often threatens to snap, but never fairly breaks the link; so that, starting at any point, an hour's easy stroll will bring you back to your station. I have quite lost my heart to this charming creation, and there are so many things to be said about it that I hardly know where to begin. The great fact, I suppose, is that it contains a Roman substructure, rests for much of its course on foundations laid by that race of master-builders. But in spite of this sturdy origin, much of which is buried in the well-trodden soil of the ages, it is the gentlest and least offensive of ramparts; it completes its long irregular curve without a frown or menace in all its disembattled stretch. The earthy deposit of time has, indeed, in some places climbed so high about its base that it amounts to no more than a causeway of modest dimensions. It has everywhere, however, a rugged outer parapet and a broad hollow flagging, wide enough for two strollers abreast. Thus equipped, it wanders through its adventurous circuit; now sloping, now bending, now broadening into a terrace, now narrowing into an alley, now swelling into an arch, now dipping into steps, now passing some thorn-screened garden, and now reminding you that it was once a more serious matter than all this by the extrusion of a rugged, ivy-smothered tower. Its final hoary humility is enhanced, to your mind, by the freedom with which you may approach it from any point in the town. Every few steps, as you go, you see some little court or alley boring toward it through the close-pressed houses. It is full of that delightful element of the crooked, the accidental, the unforeseen, which, to American eyes, accustomed to our eternal straight lines and right angles, is the striking feature of European street scenery. An American strolling in the Chester streets finds a perfect

3

feast of crookedness – of those random corners, projec-
tions and recesses, odd domestic interspaces charmingly
saved or lost, those innumerable architectural surprises
and caprices and fantasies which lead to such refreshing
exercise a vision benumbed by brownstone fronts. An
American is born to the idea that on his walks abroad it
is perpetual level wall ahead of him, and such a revelation
as he finds here of infinite accident and infinite effect
gives a wholly novel zest to the use of his eyes. It
produces, too, the reflection – a superficial and fallacious
one perhaps – that amid all this cunning chiaroscuro of
its *mise en scène*, life must have more of a certain homely
entertainment. It is at least no fallacy to say that childhood – or the later memory of childhood – must borrow
from such a background a kind of anecdotical wealth.
We all know how in the retrospect of later moods the
incidents of early youth 'compose', visibly, each as an
individual picture, with a magic for which the greatest
painters have no corresponding art. There is a vivid
reflection of this magic in some of the early pages of
Dickens' 'Copperfield' and of George Eliot's 'Mill on the
Floss', the writers having had the happiness of growing
up among old, old things. Two or three of the phases of
this rambling wall belong especially to the class of things
fondly remembered. In one place it skirts the edge of
the cathedral graveyard, and sweeps beneath the great
square tower and behind the sacred east window of the
choir. Of the cathedral there is more to say; but just the
spot I speak of is the best standpoint for feeling how fine
an influence in the architectural line – where theoretic-
ally, at least, influences are great – is the massive tower

of an English abbey, dominating the homes of men; and for watching the eddying flight of swallows make vaster still to the eye the large calm fields of stonework. At another point, two battered and crumbling towers, decaying in their winding-sheets of ivy, make a prodigiously designed diversion. One inserted in the body of the wall and the other connected with it by a short crumbling ridge of masonry, they contribute to a positive jumble of local colour. A shaded mall wanders at the foot of the rampart; beside this passes a narrow canal, with locks and barges and burly watermen in smocks and breeches; while the venerable pair of towers, with their old red sandstone sides peeping through the gaps in their green mantles, rest on the soft grass of one of those odd fragments of public garden, a crooked strip of ground turned to social account, which one meets at every turn, apparently, in England – a tribute to the needs of the 'masses'. *Stat magni nominis umbra*. The quotation is doubly pertinent here, for this little garden-strip is adorned with mossy fragments of Roman stonework, bits of pavement, altars, baths, disinterred in the local soil. England is the land of small economies, and the present rarely fails to find good use for the odds and ends of the past. These two hoary shells of masonry are therefore converted into 'museums', receptacles for the dustiest and shabbiest of tawdry back-parlour curiosities. Here preside a couple of those grotesque creatures, *à la* Dickens, whom one finds squeezed into every cranny of English civilisation, scraping a thin subsistence, like mites in a mouldy cheese.

Next after its wall – possibly even before it – Chester

values its Rows, an architectural idiosyncrasy which must be seen to be appreciated. They are a sort of Gothic edition of the blessed arcades and porticoes of Italy, and consist, roughly speaking, of a running public passage tunnelled through the second storey of the houses. The low basement is thus directly on the drive-way, to which a flight of steps descends, at frequent intervals, from this superincumbent verandah. The upper portion of the houses projects to the outer line of the gallery, where they are propped with pillars and posts and parapets. The shop-fronts face along the arcade and admit you to little caverns of traffic, more or less dusky according to their opportunities for illumination in the rear. If the picturesque be measured by its hostility to our modern notions of convenience, Chester is probably the most romantic city in the world. This arrangement is end-lessly rich in opportunities for amusing effect, but the full charm of the architecture of which it is so essential a part must be observed from the street below. Chester is still an antique town, and mediaeval England sits bravely under her gables. Every third house is a 'speci-men' – gabled and latticed, timbered and carved, and wearing its years more or less lightly. These ancient dwellings present every shade and degree of historical colour and expression. Some are dark with neglect and deformity, and the horizontal slit admitting light into the lurking Row seems to collapse on its dislocated props like a pair of toothless old jaws. Others stand there square-shouldered and sturdy, with their beams painted and straightened, their plaster whitewashed, their carv-ings polished, and the low casement covering the breadth of the frontage adorned with curtains and flower-pots. It is noticeable that the actual townsfolk have bravely accepted the situation bequeathed by the past, and the large number of rich and intelligent restorations of the old façades makes an effective jumble of their piety and their policy. These elaborate and ingenious repairs attest a highly informed consciousness of the pictorial value of the city. I indeed suspect much of this revived innocence of having recovered a freshness that never can have been, of having been restored with usurious interest. About the genuine antiques there would be properly a great deal to say, for they are really a theme for the philosopher; but the theme is too heavy for my pen, and I can give them but the passing tribute of a sigh. They are cruelly quaint, dreadfully expressive. Fix one of them with your gaze, and it seems fairly to reek with mortality. Every stain and crevice seems to syllable some human record – a record of lives airless and unlighted. I have been trying hard to fancy them animated by the children of 'Merry England', but I am quite unable to think of them save as peopled by the victims of dismal old-world pains and fears. Human life, surely, packed away behind those impenetrable lattices of lead and bottle-glass, just above which the black outer beam marks the suffocating nearness of the ceiling, can have expanded into scant freedom and bloomed into small sweetness.

Nothing has struck me more in my strolls along the Rows than the fact that the most zealous observation can keep but uneven pace with the fine differences in national manners. Some of the most sensible of these differences are yet so subtle and indefinable that one must give up the attempt to express them, though the omission leave but a rough sketch. As you pass with the bustling current from shop to shop, you feel local custom and tradition – another tone of things – pressing on you from every side. The tone of things is somehow heavier than with us; manners and modes are more absolute and positive; they seem to swarm and to thicken the atmosphere about you. Morally and physically it is a denser air than ours. We seem loosely hung together at home as compared with the English, every man of whom is a tight fit in his place. It is not an inferential but a palpable fact that England is a crowded country. There is stillness and space – grassy, oak-studded space – at Eaton Hall, where the Marquis of Westminster dwells (or I believe can afford to humour his notion of not dwelling), but there is a crowd and a hubbub in Chester. Wherever you go the population has overflowed. You stroll on the walls at eventide and you hardly find elbow-room. You haunt the cathedral shades, and a dozen sauntering mortals temper your solitude. You glance up an alley or side-street, and discover populous windows and doorsteps. You roll along country roads and find countless humble pedestrians dotting the green way-sides. The English landscape is always a 'landscape with figures'. And everywhere you go you are accompanied by a vague consciousness of the British child hovering about your knees and coat-skirts, naked, grimy, and portentous. You reflect with a sort of physical relief on Australia, Canada, India. Where there are many men, of course, there are many needs; which helps to justify to the philosophic stranger the vast number and the irresistible coquetry of the little shops which adorn these low-browed Rows. The shop-fronts have always seemed to me the most elegant things in England; and I waste more time than I should care to confess to in covetous contemplation of the vast, clear panes behind which the nether integuments of gentlemen are daintily suspended from glittering brass rods. The manners of the dealers in these comfortable wares seldom fail to confirm your agreeable impression. You are thanked with effusion for expending twopence – a fact of deep significance to the truly analytic mind, and which always seems to me a vague reverberation from certain of Miss Edgeworth's novels, perused in childhood. When you think of the small profits, the small jealousies, the long waiting, and the narrow margin for evil days implied by this redundancy of shops and shopmen, you hear afresh the steady rumble of that deep keynote of English manners, over-scored so often, and with such sweet beguilement, by finer harmonies, but never extinguished – the economic struggle for existence.

The Rows are as 'scenic' as one could wish, and it is a pity that before the birth of their modern consciousness there was no English Balzac to introduce them into a realistic romance with a psychological commentary. But the cathedral is better still, modestly as it stands on the roll of English abbeys. It is of moderate dimensions, and rather meagre in form and ornament; but to an American it expresses and answers for the type, producing thereby the proper vibrations. Among these is a certain irresistible regret that so much of its hoary substance should give place to the fine, fresh-coloured masonry with which

Mr Gilbert Scott, ruthless renovator, is so intelligently investing it. The red sandstone of the primitive structure, darkened and devoured by time, survives at many points in frowning mockery of the imputed need of tinkering. The great tower, however – completely restored – rises high enough to seem to belong, as cathedral towers should, to the far-off air that vibrates with the chimes and the swallows, and to square serenely, east and west and south and north, its embossed and fluted sides. English cathedrals, within, are apt at first to look pale and naked; but after a while, if the proportions be fair and the spaces largely distributed, when you perceive the light beating softly down from the cold clerestory and your eye measures caressingly the tallness of columns and the hollowness of arches, and lingers on the old genteel inscriptions of mural marbles and brasses; and, above all, when you become conscious of that sweet, cool mustiness in the air which seems to haunt these places as the very climate of Episcopacy, you may grow to feel that they are less the empty shells of a departed faith than the abodes of a faith which may still affirm a presence and awaken echoes. Catholicism has gone, but Anglicanism has the next best music. So at least it seemed to me, a Sunday or two since, as I sat in the choir at Chester awaiting a discourse from Canon Kingsley. The Anglican service had never seemed to my profane sense so much an affair of magnificent intonations and cadences – of pompous effects of resonance and melody. The vast oaken architecture of the stalls among which we nestled – somewhat stiffly and with a due apprehension of wounded ribs and knees – climbing vainly against the dizzier reach of the columns; the beautiful English voices of certain officiating canons; the little rosy 'king's scholars' sitting ranged beneath the pulpit, in white-winged surplices, which made their heads, above the pew-edges, look like rows of sleepy cherubs: every element in the scene gave it a great spectacular beauty. They suggested too what is suggested in England at every turn, that conservatism here has all the charm and leaves dissent and democracy and other vulgar variations nothing but their bald logic. Conservatism has the cathedrals, the colleges, the castles, the gardens, the traditions, the associations, the fine names, the better manners, the poetry; Dissent has the dusky brick chapels in provincial by-streets, the names out of Dickens, the uncertain tenure of the *h*, and the poor *mens sibi conscia recti*. Differences which in other countries are slight and varying, almost metaphysical, as one may say, are marked in England by a gulf. Nowhere else does the degree of one's respectability involve such solid consequences, and I am sure I don't wonder that the sacramental word which with us (and, in such correlatives as they possess, more or less among the continental races) is pronounced lightly and facetiously and as a quotation from the Philistines, is uttered here with a perfectly grave face. To have the courage of one's mere convictions is in short to have a prodigious deal of courage, and I think one must need as much to be a Dissenter as one needs patience not to be a duke. Perhaps the Dissenters (to limit the question to them) manage to stay out of the church by letting it all hang on the sermon. Canon Kingsley's discourse was one more example of the familiar truth – not without its significance to minds zealous for the good old fashion of 'making an effort' – that there is an odd link between large forms and small emanations. The sermon, beneath that triply consecrated vault, should have had a builded majesty. It had not; and I confess that a tender memory of ancient obligations to the author of 'Westward Ho!' and 'Hypatia' forbids my saying more of it. An American, I think, is not incapable of taking a secret satisfaction in an incongruity of this kind. He finds with relief that even mortals reared as in the ring of a perpetual circus are only mortals. His constant sense of the beautiful scenic properties of English life is apt to beget a habit of melancholy reference to the dead-blank wall which forms the background of our own life-drama; and from doubting in this fantastic humour whether we have even that modest value in the scale of beauty that he has sometimes fondly hoped, he lapses into a moody scepticism as to our place in the scale of 'importance', and finds himself wondering vaguely whether this be not a richer race as well as a lovelier land. That of course will never do; so that when after being escorted down the beautiful choir in what, from the American point of view, is an almost gorgeous ecclesiastical march, by the Dean in a white robe trimmed with scarlet and black-robed sacristans carrying silver wands, the officiating canon mounts into a splendid canopied and pinnacled pulpit of Gothic stone-work and proves – not an 'acting' Jeremy Taylor, our poor sentimental tourist begins to hold up his head again and to reflect that so far as we *have* opportunities we mostly rise to them. I am not sure indeed that in the excess of his reaction he is not tempted to accuse his English neighbours of being impenetrable and uninspired, to affirm that they do not half discern their good fortune, and that it takes passionate pilgrims, vague aliens and other disinherited persons to appreciate the 'points' of this admirable country.

Lichfield and Warwick

To write at Oxford of anything but Oxford requires, on the part of the sentimental tourist, no small power of mental abstraction. Yet I have it at heart to pay to three or four other scenes recently visited the debt of an enjoyment hardly less profound than my relish for this scholastic paradise. First among these is the cathedral city of Lichfield – the city, I say, because Lichfield has a character of its own apart from its great ecclesiastical feature. In the centre of its little market-place – dullest and sleepiest of provincial market-places – rises a huge effigy of Dr Johnson, the *genius loci*, who was constructed, humanly, with very nearly as large an architecture as the great abbey. The Doctor's statue, which is of some inexpensive composite painted a shiny brown, and of no great merit of design, fills out the vacant dulness of the little square in much the same way as his massive personality occupies – with just a margin for Garrick – the record of his native town. In one of the volumes of Croker's 'Boswell' is a steel plate of the old Johnsonian birth-house, by the aid of a vague recollection of which I detected the dwelling beneath its modernised frontage. It bears no mural inscription and, save for a hint of antiquity in the receding basement, with pillars supporting the floor above, seems in no especial harmony with Johnson's time or fame. Lichfield in general appeared to me indeed to have little to say about her great son beyond the fact that the smallness and the sameness and the dulness, amid which it is so easy to fancy a great intellectual appetite turning sick with inanition, may help to explain the Doctor's subsequent almost ferocious fondness for London. I walked about the silent streets, trying to repeople them with wigs and short-clothes, and, while I lingered near the cathedral, endeavoured to guess the message of its Gothic graces to Johnson's ponderous classicism. But I achieved but a colourless picture at the best, and the most vivid image in my mind's eye was that of the London coach facing towards Temple Bar with the young author of 'Rasselas' scowling near-sightedly from the cheapest seat. With him goes the interest of Lichfield town. The place is stale without being really antique. It is as if that prodigious temperament had absorbed and appropriated its original vitality.

If every dull provincial town, however, formed but a girdle of quietude to a cathedral as rich as that of Lichfield, one would thank it for letting one alone. Lichfield Cathedral is great among churches, and bravely performs the prime duty of objects of its order – that of seeming for the time (to minds unsophisticated by architectural culture) the finest, on the whole, of all such objects. This one is rather oddly placed, on the slope of a hill, the particular spot having been chosen, I believe, because sanctified by the sufferings of certain primitive martyrs; but it is fine to see how its upper portions surmount any crookedness of posture and its great towers overtake in mid-air the conditions of perfect symmetry. The close is extraordinarily attractive; a long sheet of water expands behind it and, besides leading the eye off into a sweet green landscape, renders the inestimable service of reflecting the three spires as they rise above the great trees which mask the Palace and the Deanery. These august abodes edge the northern side of the slope, and behind their huge gate-posts and close-wrought gates the atmosphere of the Georgian era seems to abide. Before them stretches a row of huge elms, which must have been old when Johnson was young; and between these and the long-buttressed wall of the cathedral, you may stroll to and fro among as pleasant a mixture of influences (I imagine) as any in England. You can stand back here, too, from the west front further than in many cases, and examine at your ease its lavish decoration. You are perhaps a trifle too much at your ease; for you soon discover what a more cursory glance might not betray, that the immense façade has been covered with stucco and paint, that an effigy of Charles II, in wig and plumes and trunk-hose, of almost Gothic grotesqueness, surmounts the middle window; that the various other statues of saints and kings have but recently climbed into their niches; and that the whole expanse is in short an imposture. All this was done some fifty years ago, in the taste of that day as to restoration, and yet it but partially mitigates the impressiveness of the high façade, with its brace of spires, and the great embossed and image-fretted surface, to which the lowness of the portals (the too frequent reproach of English abbeys) seems to give a loftier reach. Passing beneath one of these low portals, however, I found myself gazing down as noble a church vista as any you need desire. The cathedral is of magnificent length, and the screen between nave and choir has been removed, so that from stem to stern, as one may say, of the great vessel of the church, it is all a mighty avenue of multitudinous slender columns, terminating in what seems a great screen of ruby and sapphire and topaz – one of the finest east windows in England. The cathedral is narrow in proportion to its length; it is the long-drawn aisle of the poet in perfection, and there is something grandly elegant in the unity of effect produced by this unobstructed perspective. The charm is increased by a singular architectural fantasy. Standing in the centre of the doorway, you perceive that the eastern wall does not directly face you, and that from the beginning of the choir the receding aisle deflects slightly to the left, in reported suggestion of the droop of the Saviour's head on the cross. Here again Mr Gilbert Scott has lately laboured to no small purpose of *un*doing, it would appear – undoing the misdeeds of the last century. This extraordinary period expended an incalculable amount of imagination in proving that it had none. Universal whitewash was the least of its offences. But this has been scraped away and the solid stonework left to speak for itself, the delicate capitals and cornices disencrusted and discreetly rechiselled and the whole temple aesthetically rededicated. Its most beautiful feature, happily, has needed no repair, for its perfect beauty has been its safeguard. The great choir window of Lichfield is the noblest glass-work before the spell of which one's soul has become simple. I remember nowhere colours so chaste and grave, and yet so rich and true, or a cluster of designs so piously decorative and yet so vivified. Such

a window as this seems to me the most scared ornament of a great church; to be, not like vault and screen
and altar, the dim contingent promise to the spirit,
but the very redemption of the whole vow. This Lichfield glass is not the less interesting for being visibly of
foreign origin. Exceeding so obviously as it does the
range of English genius in this line, it indicates at least
the heavenly treasure stored up in continental churches.
It dates from the early sixteenth century, and was transferred hither sixty years ago from a decayed Belgian
abbey. This, however, is not all of Lichfield. You have
not seen it till you have strolled and re-strolled along
the close on every side, and watched the three spires
constantly change their relation as you move and pause.
Nothing can well be finer than the combination of the
two lesser ones soaring equally in front with the third
riding tremendously the magnificently sustained line of
the roof. At a certain distance against the sky this long
ridge seems something infinite and the great spire to sit
astride of it like a giant mounted on a mastodon. Your
sense of the huge mass of the building is deepened by
the fact that though the central steeple is of double the
elevation of the others, you see it, from some points,
borne back in a perspective which drops it to half their
stature and lifts them into immensity. But it would take
long to tell all that one sees and fancies and thinks in
a lingering walk about so great a church as this.

To walk in quest of any object that one has more or
less tenderly dreamed of, to find your way, to steal upon
it softly, to see at last, if it be church or castle, the
tower-tops peeping above elms or beeches – to push

forward with a rush, and emerge and pause and draw
that first long breath which is the compromise between
so many sensations: this is a pleasure left to the tourist
even after the broad glare of photography has dissipated
so many of the sweet mysteries of travel; even in a
season when he is fatally apt to meet a dozen fellow
pilgrims returning from the shrine, each as big a fool, so
to speak, as he ever was, or to overtake a dozen more
telegraphing their impressions down the line as they
arrive. Such a pleasure I lately enjoyed quite in its perfection, in a walk to Haddon Hall, along a meadow-path
by the Wye, in this interminable English twilight which
I am never weary of admiring watch in hand. Haddon
Hall lies among Derbyshire hills, in a region infested, I
was about to write, by Americans. But I achieved my
own sly pilgrimage in perfect solitude; and as I descried
the gray walls among the rook-haunted elms I felt not
like a dusty tourist, but like a successful adventurer. I
have certainly had, as a dusty tourist, few more charming
moments than some – such as any one, I suppose, is free
to have – that I passed on a little ruined gray bridge
which spans, with its single narrow arch, a trickling
stream at the base of the eminence from which those
walls and trees look down. The twilight deepened, the
ragged battlements and the low, broad oriels glanced
duskily from the foliage, the rooks wheeled and clam-
oured in the glowing sky; and if there had been a ghost
on the premises I certainly ought to have seen it. In
fact I did see it, as we see ghosts nowadays. I felt the
incommunicable spirit of the scene with the last, the
right intensity. The old life, the old manners, the old

figures seemed present again. The great *coup de théâtre* of the young woman who shows you the Hall – it is rather languidly done on her part – is to point out a little dusky door opening from a turret to a back terrace as the aperture through which Dorothy Vernon eloped with Lord John Manners. I was ignorant of this episode, for I was not to enter the place till the morrow, and I am still unversed in the history of the actors. But as I stood in the luminous dusk weaving the romance of the spot, I recognised the inevitability of a Dorothy Vernon and quite understood a Lord John. It was of course on just such an evening that the romantic event came off, and by listening with the proper credulity, I might surely hear on the flags of the castle court ghostly footfalls and feel in their movements the old heart-beats. The only footfall I can conscientiously swear to, however, is the far from spectral tread of the damsel who led me through the mansion in the prosier light of the next morning. Haddon Hall, I believe, is one of the sights in which it is the fashion to be 'disappointed'; a fact explained in a great measure by the absence of a formal approach to the house, which shows its low, gray front to every trudger on the high-road. But the charm of the spot is so much less that of grandeur than that of melancholy, that it is rather deepened than diminished by this attitude of obvious survival and decay. And for that matter, when you have entered the steep little outer court through the huge thickness of the low gateway, the present seems effactually walled out and the past walled in, even as a dead man in a sepulchre. It is very dead, of a fine June morning, the genius of Haddon Hall; and the silent courts and chambers, with their hues of ashen gray and faded brown, seem as time-bleached as the dry bones of any mouldering mortality. The comparison is odd, but Haddon Hall reminded me perversely of some of the larger houses at Pompeii. The private life of the past is revealed in each case with very much the same distinctness and on a scale small enough not to stagger the imagination. This old dwelling, indeed, has so little of the mass and expanse of the classic feudal castle that it almost suggests one of those miniature models of great buildings which lurk in dusty corners of museums. But it is large enough to be delectably complete and to contain an infinite store of the poetry of grass-grown courts looked into by wide, jutting windows and climbed out of by crooked stone stairways mounting against the walls to little high-placed doors. The 'tone' of Haddon Hall, of all its walls and towers and stonework, is the gray of unpolished silver, and the reader who has been in England need hardly be reminded of the sweet accord – to eye and mind alike – existing between all stony surfaces covered with the pale corrosions of time and the deep living green of the strong ivy which seems to feed on their slow decay. Of this effect and of a hundred others – from those that belong to low-browed, stone-paved empty rooms where life was warm and atmospheres thick, to those one may note where the dark tower stairway emerges at last, on a level with the highest beech-tops, against the cracked and sun-baked parapet which flaunted the castle standard over the castle woods – of every form of sad desuetude and picturesque decay Haddon Hall contains some delightful example. Its finest point is undoubtedly a certain court from which a stately flight of steps ascends to the terrace where that daughter of the Vernons whom I have mentioned took such happy thought for our requiring, as the phrase is, a reference. These steps, with the terrace, its balustrade topped with great ivy-muffled knobs of stone and its high background of massed woods, form the ideal *mise en scène* for portions of Shakespeare's comedies. 'It's exactly Elizabethan,' said my companion. Here the Countess Olivia may have listened to the fantastic Malvolio, or Beatrix, superbest of flirts, have come to summon Benedick to dinner.

The glories of Chatsworth, which lies but a few miles from Haddon, serve as a marked offset to its more delicate merits, just as they are supposed to gain, I believe, in the tourist's eyes, by contrast with its charming, its almost Italian shabbiness. But the glories of Chatsworth, incontestable as they are, were so effectually eclipsed to my mind, a couple of days later, that in future, when I think of an English mansion, I shall think only of Warwick, and when I think of an English park, only of Blenheim. Your run by train through the gentle Warwickshire land does much to prepare you for the great spectacle of the castle, which seems hardly more than a sort of massive symbol and synthesis of the broad prosperity and peace and leisure diffused over this great pastoral expanse. The Warwickshire meadows are to common English scenery what this is to that of the rest of the world. For mile upon mile you can see nothing but broad sloping pastures of velvet turf, overbrowsed by sheep of the most fantastic shagginess, and garnished with hedges out of the trailing luxury of whose verdure great ivy-tangled oaks and elms arise with a kind of architectural regularity. The landscape indeed sins by excess of nutritive suggestion; it savours of larder and manger; it is too ovine, too bovine, it is almost asinine; and if you were to believe what you see before you this rugged globe would be a sort of boneless ball covered with some such plush-like integument as might be figured by the down on the cheek of a peach. But a great thought keeps you company as you go and gives character to the scenery. Warwickshire – you say it over and over – was Shakespeare's county. Those who think that a great genius is something supremely ripe and healthy and human may find comfort in the fact. It helps greatly to enliven my own vague conception of Shakespeare's temperament, with which I find it no great shock to be obliged to associate ideas of mutton and beef. There is something as final, as disillusioned of the romantic horrors of rock and forest, as deeply attuned to human needs in the Warwickshire pastures as there is in the underlying morality of the poet.

With human needs in general Warwick Castle may be in no great accord, but few places are more gratifying to the sentimental tourist. It is the only great residence he may have coveted as a home. The fire that we heard so much of last winter in America appears to have consumed but an inconsiderable and easily spared portion of the house, and the great towers rise over the great trees and the town with the same grand air as before. Picturesquely, Warwick gains from not being sequestered, after the common fashion, in acres of park.

The village street winds about the garden walls, though its hum expires before it has had time to scale them. There can be no better example of the way in which stone walls, if they do not of necessity make a prison, may on occasions make a palace, than the prodigious privacy maintained thus about a mansion whose windows and towers form the main feature of a bustling town. At Warwick the past joins hands so stoutly with the present that you can hardly say where one begins and the other ends, and you rather miss the various crannies and gaps of what I just now called the Italian shabbiness of Haddon. There is a Caesar's tower and a Guy's tower and half a dozen more, but they are so well-conditioned in their ponderous antiquity that you are at a loss whether to consider them parts of an old house revived or of a new house picturesquely superannuated. Such as they are, however, plunging into the grassed and gravelled courts from which their battlements look really feudal, and into gardens large enough for all delight and too small, as they should be, to be amazing; and with ranges between them of great apartments at whose hugely recessed windows you may turn from Vandyck and Rembrandt to glance down the cliff-like pile into the Avon, washing the base like a lordly moat, with its bridge, and its trees and its memories, they mark the very model of a great hereditary dwelling – one which amply satisfies the imagination without irritating the democratic conscience. The pictures at Warwick reminded me afresh of an old conclusion on this matter; that the best fortune for good pictures is not to be crowded into public collections – not even into the relative privacy of Salons Carrés and Tribunes – but to hang in largely spaced half-dozens on the walls of fine houses. Here the historical atmosphere, as one may call it, is almost a compensation for the often imperfect light. If this be true of most pictures it is especially so of the works of Vandyck, whom you think of, wherever you may find him, as having, with that thorough good-breeding which is the stamp of his manner, taken account in his painting of the local conditions and predestined his picture to just the spot where it hangs. This is in fact an illusion as regards the Vandycks at Warwick, for none of them represent members of the house. The very finest perhaps after the great melancholy, picturesque Charles I – death, or at least the presentiment of death on the pale horse – is a portrait from the Brignole palace at Genoa; a beautiful noble matron in black, with her little son and heir. The last Vandycks I had seen were the noble company this lady had left behind her in the Genoese palace, and as I looked at her I thought of her mighty change of circumstance. Here she sits in the mild light of midmost England; there you could almost fancy her blinking in the great glare sent up from the Mediterranean. Intensity for intensity – intensity of situation constituted – I hardly know which to choose.

North Devon

For those fanciful observers to whom broad England means chiefly the perfection of the rural picturesque, Devonshire means the perfection of England. I, at least, had so complacently taken for granted here all the characteristic graces of English scenery, had built so boldly on their rank orthodoxy, that before we fairly crossed the border I had begun to look impatiently from the carriage window for the veritable landscape in water-colours. Devonshire meets you promptly in all its purity, for the course of ten minutes you have been able to glance down the green vista of a dozen Devonshire lanes. On huge embankments of moss and turf, smothered in wild flowers and embroidered with the finest lace-work of trailing ground-ivy, rise solid walls of flowering thorn and glistening holly and golden broom, and more strong, homely shrubs than I can name, and toss their blooming tangle to a sky which seems to look down between them, in places, from but a dozen inches of blue. They are oversown with lovely little flowers with names as delicate as their petals of gold and silver and azure – bird's-eye and king's-finger and wandering-sailor – and their soil, a superb dark red, turns in spots so nearly to crimson that you almost fancy it some fantastic compound purchased at the chemist's and scattered there for ornament. The mingled reflection of this rich-hued earth and the dim green light which filters through the hedge is a masterpiece of produced beauty. A Devonshire cottage is no less striking an outcome of the ages and the seasons and the manners. Crushed beneath its burden of thatch, coated with a rough white stucco of a tone to delight a painter, nestling in deep foliage and garnished at door-step and wayside with various forms of chubby infancy, it seems to have been stationed there for no more obvious purpose than to keep a promise to your fancy, though it covers, I suppose, not a little of the sordid side of life which the fancy likes to slur over.

I rolled past lanes and cottages to Exeter, where I had counted upon the cathedral. When one has fairly tasted of the pleasure of cathedral-hunting the approach to each new possible prize of the chase gives a peculiarly agreeable zest to the curiosity. You are making a collection of great impressions, and I think the process is in no case so delightful as applied to cathedrals. Going from one fine picture to another is certainly good; but the fine pictures of the world are terribly numerous, and they have a troublesome way of crowding and jostling each other in the memory. The number of cathedrals is small, and the mass and presence of each specimen great, so that as they rise in the mind in individual majesty they dwarf all the commoner impressions of calculated effect. They form indeed but a gallery of vaster pictures; for when time has dulled the recollection of details you retain a single broad image of the vast gray edifice, with its head and shoulders, its vessel and its towers, its tone of colour, and its still green precinct. All this is especially true perhaps of one's sense of English sacred piles, which

are almost alone in possessing, as pictures, a spacious
and harmonious setting. The cathedral stands supreme,
but the close makes, always, the *scene*. Exeter is not one
of the grandest, but, in common with great and small, it
has certain points in favour of which local learning
discriminates. Exeter indeed does itself injustice by a
low, dark front, which not only diminishes the apparent
altitude of the nave, but conceals, as you look eastward,
two noble Norman towers. The front, however, which
has a gloomy impressiveness, is redeemed by two fine
features: a magnificent rose-window, whose vast stone
ribs (inclosing some very pallid last-century glass) are
disposed with the most charming intricacy; and a long
sculptured screen – a sort of stony band of images –
which traverses the façade from side to side. The little
broken-visaged effigies of saints and kings and bishops,
niched in tiers along this hoary wall, are prodigiously
black and quaint and primitive in expression; and as you
look at them with whatever contemplative tenderness
your trade of hard-working tourist may have left at your
disposal, you fancy that they are broodingly conscious
of their names, histories and misfortunes; that, sensitive
victims of time, they feel the loss of their noses, their
toes, and their crowns; and that, when the long June
twilight turns at last to a deeper gray and the quiet of
the close to a deeper stillness, they begin to peer sidewise
out of their narrow recesses and to converse in some
strange form of early English, as rigid, yet as candid, as
their features and postures, moaning, like a company of
ancient paupers round a hospital fire, over their aches
and infirmities and losses, and the sadness of being so

terribly old. The vast square transeptal towers of the church seem to me to have the same sort of personal melancholy. Nothing in all architecture expresses better, to my imagination, the sadness of survival, the resignation of dogged material continuance, than a broad expanse of Norman stonework, roughly adorned with its low relief of short columns and round arches and almost barbarous hatchet-work, and lifted high into that mild English light which accords so well with its dull gray surface. The especial secret of the impressiveness of such a Norman tower I cannot pretend to have discovered. It lies largely in the look of having been proudly and sturdily built – as if the masons had been urged by a trumpet-blast, and the stones squared by a battle-axe – contrasted with this mere idleness of antiquity and passive lapse into quaintness. A Greek temple preserves a kind of fresh immortality in its concentrated refinement, and a Gothic cathedral in its adventurous exuberance; but a Norman tower stands up like some simple strong man in his might, bending a melancholy brow upon an age which demands that strength shall be cunning.

The North Devon coast, whither it was my design on coming to Exeter to proceed, has the primary merit of being, as yet, virgin soil as to railways. I went accordingly from Barnstaple to Ilfracombe on the top of a coach, in the fashion of elder days; and, thanks to my position, I managed to enjoy the landscape in spite of the two worthy aboriginals before me who were reading aloud together, with a natural glee which might have passed for fiendish malice, the *Daily Telegraph*'s painfully vivid account of the defeat of the Atalanta crew. It seemed to me, I remember, a sort of pledge and token of the invincibility of English muscle that a newspaper record of its prowess should have power to divert my companions' eyes from the bosky flanks of Devonshire combes. The little watering-place of Ilfracombe is seated at the lower verge of one of these seaward-plunging valleys, between a couple of magnificent headlands which hold it in a hollow slope and offer it securely to the caress of the Bristol Channel. It is a very finished little specimen of its genus, and I think that during my short stay there I expended as much attention on its manners and customs and its social physiognomy as on its cliffs and beach and great coast-view. My chief conclusion perhaps, from all these things, was that the terrible 'summer question' which works annual anguish in so many American households would rage less hopelessly if we had a few Ilfracombes scattered along our Atlantic coast; and furthermore that the English are masters of the art of not losing sight of ease and convenience in the pursuit of the pastoral life – unlike our own people, who, when seeking rural beguilement, are apt but to find a new rudeness added to nature. It is just possible that at Ilfracombe ease and convenience weigh down the scale; so very substantial are they, so very officious and business-like. On the left of the town (to give an example) one of the great cliffs I have mentioned rises in a couple of massive peaks and presents to the sea an almost vertical face, all muffled in tufts of golden broom and mighty fern. You have not walked fifty yards away from the hotel before you encounter half a dozen little sign-boards, directing your steps to a path up the cliff. You follow their indications and you arrive at a little gatehouse, with photographs and various local gimcracks exposed for sale. A most respectable person appears, demands a penny and, on receiving it, admits you with great civility to commune with nature. You detect, however, various little influences hostile to perfect communion. You are greeted by another sign-board threatening legal pursuit if you attempt to evade the payment of the sacramental penny. The path, winding in a hundred ramifications over the cliff, is fastidiously solid and neat, and furnished at intervals of a dozen yards with excellent benches, inscribed by knife and pencil with the names of such visitors as do not happen to have been the elderly maiden ladies who now chiefly occupy them. All this is prosaic, and you have to subtract it in a lump from the total impression before the sense of the beguilement of nature becomes distinct. Your subtraction made, a great deal assuredly remains; quite enough, I found, to give me an ample day's refreshment; for English scenery, like most other English commodities, resists and rewards familiar use. The cliffs are superb, the play of light and shade upon them is a perpetual study, and the air a particular mixture of the breath of the hills and moors and the breath of the sea. I was very glad, at the end of my climb, to have a good bench to sit upon – as one must think twice in England before measuring one's length on the grassy earth; and to be able, thanks to the smooth foot-path, to get back to the hotel in a quarter of an hour. But it occurred to me that if I were an Englishman of the period, and, after ten months of a busy London life, my fancy were turning to a holiday, to rest and change and oblivion of the ponderous social burden, it might find rather less inspiration than needful in a vision of the little paths of Ilfracombe, of the sign-boards and the penny fee and the solitude tempered by old ladies and sheep. I wondered whether change perfect enough to be salutary does not imply something more pathless, more idle, more unreclaimed from that deep-bosomed nature to which the overwrought mind reverts with passionate longing; something after all attainable at a moderate distance from New York and Boston. I must add that I cannot find in my heart to object, even on grounds the most aesthetic, to the very beautiful and excellent inn at Ilfracombe, where such of my readers as are perchance actually wrestling with the question of 'where to go' may be interested to learn that they may live *en pension*, very well indeed, at a cost of ten shillings a day. I have paid the American hotel-clerk a much heavier tax on a much lighter entertainment. I made the acquaintance at this establishment of that strange fruit of time the insular *table d'hôte*, but I confess that, faithful to the habit of a tourist open to the *arrière-pensée*, I have retained a more vivid impression of the talk and the faces than of our joints and side-dishes. I noticed here what I have often noticed before (the truth perhaps has never been duly recognised), that no people profit so eagerly as the English by the suspension of a common social law. A *table d'hôte*, being something abnormal and experimental, as it were, resulted apparently in a complete reversal of the supposed national characteristics. Conversation was universal – uproarious almost; old legends and ironies about the insular *morgue* seemed to see their ground crumble away. What social, what psychologic earth-quake, in our own time, had occurred?

These are meagre memories, however, compared with those which cluster about that place of pleasant-ness which is locally known as Lynton. I am afraid I may seem a mere professional gusher when I declare how common almost any term appears to me applied to Lynton with descriptive intent. The little village is perched on the side of one of the great mountain cliffs with which this whole coast is adorned, and on the edge of a lovely gorge through which a broad hill-torrent foams and tumbles from the great moors whose heather-crested waves rise purple along the inland sky. Below it, close beside the beach where the little torrent meets the sea, is the sister village of Lynmouth. Here – as I stood on the bridge that spans the stream and looked at the stony backs and foundations and overclambering garden verdure of certain little gray old houses which plunge their feet into it, and then up at the tender green of scrub-oak and fern, at the colour of gorse and broom and bracken climbing the sides of the hills and leaving them bare-crowned to the sun like miniature mountains – I read an unnatural blueness into the northern sea, and the village below put on the grace of one of the hundred hamlets of the Riviera. The little Castle Hotel at Lynton is a spot so consecrated to supreme repose – to sitting with a book in the terrace-garden, among blooming plants of aristocratic magnitude and rarity, and watching the finest piece of colour in all nature, the glowing red and green of the great cliffs beyond the little harbour-mouth, as they shift and change and melt, the livelong

day, from shade to shade and ineffable tone to tone –
that I feel as if in helping it to publicity I were doing it
rather a disfavour than a service. It is in fact a very deep
and sure retreat, and I have never known one where
purchased hospitality wore a more disinterested smile.
Lynton is of course a capital centre for excursions, but
two or three of which I had time to make. None is more
beautiful than a simple walk along the running face of
the cliffs to a singular rocky eminence whose curious
abutments and pinnacles of stone have caused it to be
named the Castle. It has a fantastic resemblance to some
hoary feudal ruin, with crumbling towers and gaping
chambers tenanted by wild sea-birds. The late afternoon
light had a way, at this season, of lingering on until
within a couple of hours of midnight; and I remember
among the charmed moments of English travel none of
a more vividly poetical tinge than a couple of evenings
spent on the summit of this all but legendary pile in
company with the slow-coming darkness and the short,
sharp cry of the sea-mews. There are places whose very
aspect is a story or a song. This jagged and pinnacled
coast-wall, with the rock-strewn valley behind it, the
sullen calmness of the unbroken tide at the dreadful base
of the cliffs (where they divide into low sea-caves, making
pillars and pedestals for the fantastic imagery of their
summits), prompted one to wanton reminiscence and
outbreak, to a recall of some drawing of Gustave Doré's
(of his good time), which was a divination of the place
and made one look for his signature under a stone, or,
better still, to respouting, for sympathy and relief, some
idyllic Tennysonian line that haunted one's destitute past

and that seemed to speak of the conditions in spite of being false to them geographically.

The last stage in my visit to North Devon was the long drive along the beautiful remnant of coast and through the rich pastoral scenery of Somerset. The whole broad spectacle that one dreams of viewing in a foreign land to the homely music of a postboy's whip I beheld on this admirable drive – breezy highlands clad in the warm blue-brown of heather-tufts as if in mantles of rusty velvet, little bays and coves curving gently to the doors of clustered fishing-huts, deep pastures and broad forests, villages thatched and trellised as if to take a prize for improbability, manor-tops peeping over rook-haunted avenues. I ought to make especial note of an hour I spent at midday at the village of Porlock in Somerset. Here the thatch seemed steeper and heavier, the yellow roses on the cottage walls more cunningly mated with the crumbling stucco, the dark interiors within the open doors more quaintly pictorial, than elsewhere; and as I loitered, while the horses rested, in the little cool old timber-steepled, yew-shaded church, betwixt the high-backed manorial pew and the battered tomb of a crusading knight and his lady, and listened to the simple prattle of a blue-eyed old sexton, who showed me where, as a boy, in scantier corduroys, he had scratched his name on the recumbent lady's breast, it seemed to me that this at last was old England indeed, and that in a moment more I should see Sir Roger de Coverley marching up the aisle. Certainly, to give a proper account of it all, I should need nothing less than the pen of Mr Addison.

Wells and Salisbury

The pleasantest thing in life is doubtless ever the pleasant-
ness that has found one off one's guard – though if I
was off my guard in arriving at Wells it could only have
been by the effect of a frivolous want of information. I
knew in a general way that this ancient little town had a
great cathedral to produce, but I was far from suspecting
the intensity of the impression that awaited me. The
immense predominance of the Minster towers, as you
see them from the approaching train over the clustered
houses at their feet, gives you indeed an intimation of
its character, suggests that the city is nothing if not
sanctified; but I can wish the traveller no better fortune
than to stroll forth in the early evening with as large a
reserve of ignorance as my own, and treat himself to an
hour of discoveries. I was lodged on the edge of the
cathedral lawn and had only to pass beneath one of
the three crumbling Priory gates which enclose it, and
cross the vast grassy oval, to stand before a minster-
front which ranks among the first three or four in England. Wells Cathedral is extremely fortunate in being
approached by this wide green level, on which the spectator may loiter and stroll to and fro and shift his standpoint to his heart's content. The spectator who does not
hesitate to avail himself of his privilege of unlimited
fastidiousness might indeed pronounce it too isolated

for perfect picturesqueness – too uncontrasted with the profane architecture of the human homes for which it pleads to the skies. But Wells is in fact not a city with a cathedral for central feature; it is a cathedral with a little city gathered at the base and forming hardly more than an extension of the spacious close. You feel everywhere the presence of the beautiful church; the place seems always to savour of a Sunday afternoon; and you imagine every house tenanted by a canon, a prebendary or a precentor, with 'backs' providing for choristers and vergers.

The great façade is remarkable not so much for its expanse as for its elaborate elegance. It consists of two great truncated towers, divided by a broad centre bearing, besides its rich fretwork of statues, three narrow lancet windows. The statues on this vast front are the great boast of the cathedral. They number, with the lateral figures of the towers, no less than three hundred; it seems densely embroidered by the chisel. They are disposed, in successive niches, along six main vertical shafts; the central windows are framed and divided by narrower shafts, and the wall above them rises into a pinnacled screen traversed by two superb horizontal rows. Add to these a close-running cornice of images along the line corresponding with the summit of the aisles and the tiers which complete the decoration of the towers on either side, and you have an immense system of images governed by a quaint theological order and most impressive in its completeness. Many of the little high-lodged effigies are mutilated, and not a few of the niches are empty, but the injury of time is not sufficient to diminish the noble serenity of the building. The injury of time is indeed being actively repaired, for the front is partly masked by a slender scaffolding. The props and platforms are of the most delicate structure, and look in fact as if they were meant to facilitate no more ponderous labour than a fitting-on of noses to disfeatured bishops and a rearrangement of the mantlefolds of straitlaced queens discomposed by the centuries. The main beauty of Wells Cathedral, to my mind, is not its more or less visible wealth of detail, but its singularly charming tone of colour. An even, sober, mouse-coloured gray invests it from summit to base, deepening nowhere to the melancholy black of your truly romantic Gothic, but showing as yet none of the spotty brightness of renovation. It is a wonderful fact that the great towers, from their lofty outlook, see never a factory chimney – those cloud-compelling spires which so often break the charm of the softest English horizons; and the general atmosphere of Wells seemed to me, for some reason, peculiarly luminous and sweet. The cathedral has never been discoloured by the moral malaria of a city with an independent secular life. As you turn back from its portal and glance at the open lawn before it, edged by the mild gray seventeenth-century deanery and the other dwellings, hardly less stately, which seem to reflect in their comfortable fronts the rich respectability of the church, and then up again at the beautiful clear-hued pile, you may fancy it less a temple for man's needs than a monument of his pride – less a fold for the flock than for the shepherds; a visible token that, besides the actual assortment of heavenly thrones, there is constantly on hand a 'full line' of cushioned cathedral stalls. Within the cathedral this impression is not diminished. The interior is vast and massive, but it lacks incident – the incident of monuments, sepulchres and chapels – and it is too brilliantly lighted for picturesque, as distinguished from strictly architectural, interest. Under this latter head it has, I believe, great importance. For myself, I can think of it only as I saw it from my place in the choir during afternoon service of a hot Sunday. The Bishop sat facing me, enthroned in a stately Gothic alcove and clad in his crimson band, his lawn sleeves and his lavender gloves; the canons, in their degree, with still other priestly forms, reclined comfortably in the carven stalls, and the scanty congregation fringed the broad aisle. But though scanty, the congregation was select; it was unexceptionably black-coated, bonneted and gloved. It savoured intensely in short of that inexorable gentility which the English put on with their Sunday bonnets and beavers and which fills me – as a mere taster of produced tastes – with a sort of fond reactionary remembrance of those animated bundles of rags which one sees kneeling in the churches of Italy. But even here, as taster of tastes, I found my account. You always do if you throw yourself confidently enough, in England, on the chapter of accidents. Before me and beside me sat a row of the comeliest young men, clad in black gowns and wearing on their shoulders long hoods trimmed with white fur. Who and what they were I know not, for I preferred not to learn, lest by chance they should not be so mediaeval as they looked.

My fancy found its account even better in the singular quaintness of the little precinct known as the Vicars'

Close. It directly adjoins the Cathedral Green, and you enter it beneath one of the solid old gatehouses which form so striking an element in the ecclesiastical furniture of Wells. It consists of a narrow, oblong court, bordered on each side with thirteen small dwellings, and terminating in a ruinous little chapel. Here formerly dwelt a congregation of minor priests, established in the thirteenth century to do curates' work for the canons. The little houses are very much modernised; but they retain their tall chimneys, with carven tablets in the face, their antique compactness and neatness, and a certain little sanctified air as of cells in a cloister. The place is adorably of another world and time, and, approaching it as I did in the first dimness of twilight, it looked to me, in its exaggerated perspective, like one of those conventional streets represented on the stage, down whose impossible vista the heroes and confidants of romantic comedies come swaggering arm-in-arm and hold amorous converse with heroines perched at second-story windows. But though the Vicars' Close is a curious affair enough, the great boast of Wells is its episcopal Palace. The Palace loses nothing from being seen for the first time in the kindly twilight, and from being approached with an uncautioned mind. To reach it (unless you go from within the cathedral by the cloisters), you pass out of the Green by another ancient gateway into the market-place, and thence back again through its own peculiar portal. My own first glimpse of it had all the felicity of a *coup de théâtre*. I saw within the dark archway an enclosure bedimmed at once with the shadows of trees and heightened with the glitter of water. The picture was worthy of this agreeable promise. Its main feature is the little gray-walled island on which the Palace stands, rising in feudal fashion out of a broad, clear moat, flanked with round towers and approached by a proper drawbridge. Along the outer side of the moat is a short walk beneath a row of picturesquely stunted elms; swans and ducks disport themselves in the current and ripple the bright shadows of the overclambering plants from the episcopal gardens and masses of wallflower lodged on the hoary battlements. On the evening of my visit the haymakers were at work on a great sloping field in the rear of the Palace, and the sweet perfume of the tumbled grass in the dusky air seemed all that was wanting to fix the scene for ever in the memory. Beyond the moat and within the gray walls dwells my lord Bishop, in the finest seat of all his order. The mansion dates from the thirteenth century; but, stately dwelling though it is, it occupies but a subordinate place in its own grounds. Their great ornament, picturesquely speaking, is the massive ruin of a banqueting-hall erected by a free-living mediaeval bishop and more or less demolished at the Reformation. With its still perfect towers and beautiful shapely windows, hung with those green tapestries so stoutly woven by the English climate, it is a relic worthy of being locked away behind an embattled wall. I have among my impressions of Wells, besides this picture of the moated Palace, half a dozen memories of the romantic sort, which I lack space to transcribe. The clearest impression perhaps is that of the beautiful church of St Cuthbert, of the same date as the cathedral, and in very much the same style of elegant, temperate Early

English. It wears one of the high-soaring towers for which Somersetshire is justly celebrated, as you may see from the window of the train in rolling past its almost top-heavy hamlets. The beautiful old church, surrounded with its green graveyard, and large enough to be impressive, without being too large (a great merit, to my sense) to be easily compassed by a deplorably unarchitectural eye, wore a native English expression to which certain humble figures in the foreground gave additional point. On the edge of the churchyard was a low-gabled house, before which four old men were gossiping in the eventide. Into the front of the house was inserted an antique alcove in stone, divided into three shallow little seats, two of which were occupied by extraordinary specimens of decrepitude. One of these ancient paupers had a huge protuberant forehead, and sat with a pensive air, his head gathered painfully upon his twisted shoulders and his legs resting across his crutch. The other was rubicund, blear-eyed and frightfully besmeared with snuff. Their voices were so feeble and senile that I could scarcely understand them, and only just managed to make out the answer to my inquiry of who and what they were – 'We're Still's Almshouse, sir.'

One of the lions, almost, of Wells (whence it is but five miles distant) is the ruin of the famous Abbey of Glastonbury, on which Henry VIII, in the language of our day, came down so heavily. The ancient splendour of the architecture survives but in scattered and scanty fragments, among influences of a rather inharmonious sort. It was cattle-market in the little town as I passed up the main street, and a savour of hoofs and hide seemed to accompany me through the easy labyrinth of the old arches and piers. These occupy a large back yard, close behind the street, to which you are most prosaically admitted by a young woman who keeps a wicket and sells tickets. The continuity of tradition is not altogether broken, however, for the little street of Glastonbury has rather an old-time aspect, and one of the houses at least must have seen the last of the abbots ride abroad on his mule. The little inn is a capital bit of character, and as I waited for the 'bus under its low dark archway (in something of the mood, possibly, in which a train was once waited for at Coventry), and watched the barmaid flirting her way to and fro out of the heavy-browed kitchen and among the lounging young appraisers of colts and steers and barmaids, I might have imagined that the Merry England of the Tudors had not utterly passed away. A beautiful England this must have been as well, if it contained many such abbeys as Glastonbury. Such of the ruined columns and portals and windows as still remain are of admirable design and finish. The door-ways are rich in marginal ornament – ornament within ornament, as it often is; for the dainty weeds and wild flowers overlace the antique tracery with their bright arabesques and deepen the gray of the stone-work as it brightens their bloom. The thousand flowers which grow among English ruins deserve a chapter to themselves. I owe them, as an observer, a heavy debt of satisfaction, but I am too little of a botanist to pay them in their own coin. It has often seemed to me in England that the purest enjoyment of architecture was to be had among the ruins of great buildings. In the perfect building one is rarely sure that the impression is simply architectural: it is more or less pictorial and romantic; it depends partly upon association and partly upon various accessories and details which, however they may be wrought into harmony with the architectural idea, are not part of its essence and spirit. But in so far as beauty of structure is beauty of line and curve, balance and harmony of masses and dimensions, I have seldom relished it as deeply as on the grassy nave of some crumbling church, before lonely columns and empty windows where the wild flowers were a cornice and the sailing clouds a roof. The arts certainly hang together in what they do for us. These hoary relics of Glastonbury reminded me in their broken eloquence of one of the other great ruins of the world – the *Last Supper* of Leonardo. A beautiful shadow, in each case, is all that remains; but that shadow is the soul of the artist.

Salisbury Cathedral, to which I made a pilgrimage on leaving Wells, is the very reverse of a ruin, and you take your pleasure there on very different grounds from those I have just attempted to define. It is perhaps the best-known typical church in the world, thanks to its shapely spire; but the spire is so simply and obviously fair that when you have respectfully made a note of it you have anticipated aesthetic analysis. I had seen it before and admired it heartily, and perhaps I should have done as well to let my admiration rest. I confess that on repeated inspection it grew to seem to me the least bit *banal*, or even *bête*, since I am talking French, and I began to consider whether it does not belong to the same range of art as the Apollo Belvedere or the Venus de' Medici.

I am inclined to think that if I had to live within sight of
a cathedral and encounter it in my daily comings and
goings I should grow less weary of the rugged black
front of Exeter than of the sweet perfection of Salisbury. There are people by temperament easily sated
with beauties specifically fair, and the effect of Salisbury
Cathedral architecturally is equivalent to that of flaxen
hair and blue eyes physiognomically. The other lions
of Salisbury, Stonehenge and Wilton House, I revisited
with undiminished interest. Stonehenge is rather a hack-
neyed shrine of pilgrimage. At the time of my former
visit a picnic-party was making libations of beer on the
dreadful altar-sites. But the mighty mystery of the place
has not yet been stared out of countenance; and as on
this occasion there were no picnickers we were left to
drink deep of all its ambiguities and intensities. It stands
as lonely in history as it does on the great plain whose
many-tinted green waves, as they roll away from it, seem
to symbolise the ebb of the long centuries which have left
it so portentously unexplained. You may put a hundred
questions to these rough-hewn giants as they bend in
grim contemplation of their fallen companions; but
your curiosity falls dead in the vast sunny stillness that
enshrouds them, and the strange monument, with all its
unspoken memories, becomes simply a heart-stirring
picture in a land of pictures. It is indeed immensely vague
and immensely deep. At a distance you see it standing in
a shallow dell of the plain, looking hardly larger than a
group of ten-pins on a bowling-green. I can fancy sitting
all a summer's day watching its shadows shorten and
lengthen again, and drawing a delicious contrast between

the world's duration and the feeble span of individual experience. There is something in Stonehenge almost reassuring to the nerves; if you are disposed to feel that the life of man has rather a thin surface and, that we soon get to the bottom of things, the immemorial gray pillars may serve to represent for you the pathless vaults beneath the house of history. Salisbury is indeed rich in antiquities. Wilton House, a delightful old residence of the Earls of Pembroke, contains a noble collection of Greek and Roman marbles. These are ranged round a charming cloister occupying the centre of the house, which is exhibited in the most liberal fashion. Out of the cloister opens a series of drawing-rooms hung with family portraits, chiefly by Vandyck, all of superlative merit. Among them hangs supreme, as the Vandyck *par excellence*, the famous and magnificent group of the whole Pembroke family of James I's time. This splendid work has every pictorial merit – design, colour, elegance, force and finish, and I have been vainly wondering to this hour what it needs to be the finest piece of portraiture, as it surely is one of the most ambitious, in the world. What it lacks, characteristically, in a certain uncompromising veracity, it recovers in the beautiful dignity of its position – unmoved from the stately house in which its author sojourned and wrought, familiar to the descendants of its noble originals.

Two Excursions

I

They differed greatly from each other, but there was something to be said for each. There seemed in respect to the first a high consensus as to its being a pity that any stranger should ever miss the Derby day. Every one assured me that this was the great festival of the English people and that one didn't really know them unless one had seen them at it. So much, since it had to do with horse-flesh, I could readily believe. Had not the newspapers been filled for weeks with recurrent dissertations upon the animals concerned in the ceremony? and was not the event, to the nation at large, only imperceptibly less momentous than the other great question of the day – the fate of empires and the reapportionment of the East? The space allotted to sporting intelligence in a compact, eclectic, 'intellectual' journal like the *Pall Mall Gazette*, had seemed for some time past a measure of the hold of such questions upon the native mind. These things, however, are very natural in a country in which in 'society' you are liable to make the acquaintance of some such syllogism as the following. You are seated at dinner next a foreign lady who has on her other hand a communicative gentleman through whom she is under instruction in the art of the right point-of-view for English life. I profit by their conversation and I learn that this point-of-view is apparently the saddle. 'You see, English life,' says the gentleman, 'is really English country life. It's the country that is the basis of English society. And you see, country life is – well, it's the *hunting*. It's the hunting that is at the bottom of it all.' In other words 'the hunting' is the basis of English society. Duly impressed with this explanation, the American observer is prepared for the huge proportions of the annual pilgrimage to Epsom. This pilgrimage, however, I was assured, though still well worth taking part in, is by no means so characteristic as in former days. It is now performed in a large measure by rail, and the spectacle on the road has lost many of its earlier and most of its finer features. The road has been given up more and more to the populace and the strangers and has ceased to be graced by the presence of ladies. Nevertheless, as a man and a stranger, I was strongly recommended to take it, for the return from the Derby is still, with all its abatements, a classic show.

I mounted upon a four-horse coach, a charming coach with a yellow body and handsome, clean-flanked leaders; placing myself beside the coachman, as I had been told this was the point of vantage. The coach was one of the vehicles of the new fashion – the fashion of public conveyances driven, for the entertainment of themselves and of the public, by gentlemen of leisure. On the Derby day all the coaches that start from the classic head-quarters – 'The White Horse' in Piccadilly – and stretch away from London toward a dozen different and well-selected goals, had been dedicated to the Epsom road.

The body of the vehicle is empty, as no one thinks of occupying any but one of the thirteen places on the top. On the Derby day, however, a properly laden coach carries a company of hampers and champagne-baskets in its inside places. I must add that on this occasion my companion was by exception a professional whip, who proved a friendly and amusing cicerone. Other companions there were, perched in the twelve places behind me, whose social quality I made less of a point of testing – though in the course of the expedition their various characteristics, under the influence of champagne, expanded so freely as greatly to facilitate the process. We were a society of exotics – Spaniards, Frenchmen, Germans. There were only two Britons, and these, according to my theory, were Australians – an antipodal bride and groom on a centripetal wedding-tour.

The drive to Epsom, when you get well out of London, is sufficiently pretty; but the part of it which most took my fancy was a district pre-eminently surburban – the classic community of Clapham. The vision of Clapham had been a part of the furniture of one's milder historic consciousness – the vision of its respectable common, its evangelical society, its rich drab humanity, its goodly brick mansions of the Georgian era. I now seemed really to focus these elements for the first time, and I thought them very charming. This epithet indeed scarcely applies to the evangelical society, which naturally, on the morning of the Derby day and during the desecrating progress of the Epsom revellers, was not much in the foreground. But all around the verdant if cockneyfied common are ranged commodious houses of a sober red complexion, from under whose neo-classic pediments you expect to see a mild-faced lady emerge – a lady in a cottage-bonnet and mittens, distributing tracts from a green silk satchel. It would take, however, the very ardour of the missionary among cannibals to stem the current of heterogeneous vehicles which at about this point takes up its metropolitan affluents and bears them in its rumbling, rattling tide. The concourse of wheeled conveyances of every possible order here becomes dense, and the spectacle from the top of the coach proportionately absorbing. You begin to perceive that the brilliancy of the road has in truth departed, and that a sustained high tone of appearance is not the note of the conditions. But when once you have grasped this fact your entertainment is continuous. You perceive that you are 'in' for the vulgar on an unsurpassable scale, something blatantly, unimaginably, heroically shocking to timid 'taste'; all that is necessary is to accept this situation and look out for illustrations. Beside you, before you, behind you, is the mighty London populace taking its *ébats*. You get for the first time a notion of the London population at large. It has piled itself into carts, into omnibuses, into every possible and impossible species of 'trap'. A large proportion of it is of course on foot, trudging along the perilous margin of the middle way in such comfort as may be gathered from fifteen miles' dodging of broken shins. The smaller the vehicle, the more rat-like the animal that drags it, the more numerous and ponderous its human freight; and as every one is nursing in his lap a parcel of provender as big as himself, wrapped in ragged newspaper, it is not surprising that roadside halts are frequent and that the taverns all the way to Epsom (it is wonderful how many there are) are encompassed by dense groups of dusty pilgrims, indulging liberally in refreshment for man and beast. And when I say man I must by no means be understood to exclude woman. The female contingent on the Derby day is not the least remarkable part of the London outpouring. Every one is prepared for 'larks', but the women are even more brilliantly and resolutely prepared than the men; there is no better chance to follow the range of type – not that it is to be called large – of the British female of the lower orders. The lady in question is usually not ornamental. She is useful, robust, prolific, excellently fitted to play the somewhat arduous part allotted to her in the great scheme of English civilisation, but she has not those graces which enable her to lend herself easily to the decoration of life. On smaller holidays – or on simple working-days – in London crowds, I have often thought she had points to contribute to the primary fine drawing, as to he id and shoulders, of the Briton of the two sexes as the race at large sketches them. But at Epsom she is too stout, too hot, too red, too thirsty, too boisterous, too strangely accoutred. And yet I wish to do her justice; so I must add that if there is something to which an American cannot refuse a tribute of admiration in the gross plebeian jollity of the Derby day, it is not evident why these dowdy Bacchantes should not get part of the credit of it. The striking thing, the interesting thing, both on the outward drive and on the return, was that the holiday was so frankly, heartily, good-humouredly taken. The people that of all peoples is habitually the most governed by decencies, proprieties, rigidities of conduct, was for one happy day unbuttoning its respectable straight-jacket and affirming its large and simple sense of the joy of life. In such a spectacle there was inevitably much that was unlucky and unprofitable; these things came uppermost chiefly on the return, when demoralisation was supreme, when the temperament of the people had begun really to take the air. For the rest, to be dressed with a kind of brutal gaudiness, to be very thirsty and violently flushed, to laugh perpetually at everything and at nothing, thoroughly to enjoy, in short, a momentous occasion – all this is not, in simple persons of the more susceptible sex, an unpardonable crime.

The course at Epsom is in itself very pretty, and disposed by nature herself in sympathetic prevision of the sporting passion. It is something like the crater of a volcano without the mountain. The outer rim is the course proper; the space within it is a vast, shallow, grassy concavity in which vehicles are drawn up and beasts tethered and in which the greater part of the multitude – the mountebanks, the betting-men and the myriad hangers-on of the scene – are congregated. The outer margin of the uplifted rim in question is occupied by the grand stand, the small stands, the paddock. The day was exceptionally beautiful; the charming sky was spotted over with little idle-looking, loafing, irresponsible clouds; the Epsom Downs went swelling away as greenly as in a coloured sporting-print, and the wooded uplands, in the middle distance, looked as innocent and pastoral as if they had never seen a policeman or a rowdy. The crowd that spread itself over this immense expanse was as rich representation of human life off its guard as one need see. One's first fate after arriving, if one is perched upon a coach, is to see the coach guided, by means best known to the coachman himself, through the tremendous press of vehicles and pedestrians, introduced into a precinct roped off and guarded from intrusion save under payment of a fee, and then drawn up alongside of the course, as nearly as possible opposite the grand stand and the winning-post. Here you have only to stand up in your place – on tiptoe, it is true, and with a good deal of stretching – to see the race fairly well. But I hasten to add that seeing the race is indifferent entertainment. In the first place you *don't* see it, and in the second – to be Irish on the occasion of a frolic – you perceive it to be not much worth the seeing. It may be fine in quality, but in quantity it is inappreciable. The horses and their jockeys first go dandling and cantering along the course to the starting-point, looking as insubstantial as sifted sunbeams. Then there is a long wait, during which, of the sixty thousand people present (my figures are imaginary), thirty thousand declare positively that they have started, and thirty thousand as positively deny it. Then the whole sixty thousand are suddenly resolved into unanimity by the sight of a dozen small jockey-heads whizzing along a very distant sky-line. In a shorter space of time than it takes me to write it, the whole thing is before you, and for the instant it is anything but beautiful. A dozen furiously revolving arms – pink, green, orange, scarlet, white – whacking the flanks of as many straining steeds; a glimpse of this, and the spectacle is over. The spectacle, however, is of course an infinitesimally small part of the purpose of Epsom and the interest of the Derby. The finer vibration resides presumably in having money on the affair.

When the Derby Stakes had been carried off by a horse of which I confess I am barbarous enough to have forgotten the name, I turned my back to the running, for all the world as if I too were largely 'interested', and sought entertainment in looking at the crowd. The crowd was very animated; that is the most succinct description I can give of it. The horses of course had been removed from the vehicles, so that the pedestrians were free to surge against the wheels and even to a certain extent to scale and overrun the carriages. This tendency became most pronounced when, as the mid-period of the day was reached, the process of lunching began to unfold itself and every coach-top to become the scene of a picnic. From this moment, at the Derby, demoralisation begins. I was in a position to observe it, all around me, in the most characteristic forms. The whole affair, as regards the conventional rigidities I spoke of a while since, becomes a real *dégringolade*. The shabbier pedestrians bustle about the vehicles, staring up at the lucky mortals who are perched in a kind of tormentingly near empyrean – a region in which dishes of lobster-salad are passed about and champagne-corks cleave the air like celestial meteors. There are nigger-minstrels and beggars and mountebanks and spangled persons on stilts and gipsy matrons, as genuine as possible, with glowing Oriental eyes and dropping their *h*'s; these last offer you for sixpence the promise of everything genteel in life

except the aspirate. On a coach drawn up beside the one
on which I had a place, a party of opulent young men
were passing from stage to stage of the higher beatitude
with a zeal which excited my admiration. They were
accompanied by two or three young ladies of the kind
that usually shares the choicest pleasures of youthful
British opulence – young ladies in whom nothing has
been neglected that can make a complexion superlative.
The whole party had been drinking deep, and one of the
young men, a pretty lad of twenty, had in an indiscreet
moment staggered down as best he could to the ground.
Here his cups proved too many for him, and he collapsed
and rolled over. In plain English he was beastly drunk.
It was the scene that followed that arrested my observation. His companions on the top of the coach called
down to the people herding under the wheels to pick
him up and put him away inside. These people were the
grimiest of the rabble, and a couple of men who looked
like coal-heavers out of work undertook to handle this
hapless youth. But their task was difficult; it was impossible to imagine a young man more drunk. He was a
mere bag of liquor – at once too ponderous and too
flaccid to be lifted. He lay in a helpless heap under the
feet of the crowd – the best intoxicated young man in
England. His extemporised chamberlains took him first
in one way and then in another; but he was like water
in a sieve. The crowd hustled over him; every one
wanted to see; he was pulled and shoved and fumbled.
The spectacle had a grotesque side, and this it was that
seemed to strike the fancy of the young man's comrades.
They had not done lunching, so they were unable to

bestow upon the incident the whole of that consideration which its high comicality deserved. But they did what they could. They looked down very often, glass in hand, during the half-hour that it went on, and they stinted neither their generous, joyous laughter nor their appreciative comments. Women are said to have no sense of humour; but the young ladies with the complexions did liberal justice to the pleasantry of the scene. Toward the last indeed their attention rather flagged; for even the best joke suffers by reiteration, and when you have seen a stupefied young man, infinitely bedusted, slip out of the embrace of a couple of clumsy roughs for the twentieth time, you may very properly suppose that you have arrived at the furthest limits of the ludicrous.

After the great race had been run I quitted my perch and spent the rest of the afternoon in wandering about the grassy concave I have mentioned. It was amusing and picturesque; it was just a huge Bohemian encampment. Here also a great number of carriages were stationed, freighted in like manner with free-handed youths and young ladies with gilded hair. These young ladies were almost the only representatives of their sex with pretensions to elegance; they were often pretty and always exhilarated. Gentlemen in pairs, mounted on stools, habited in fantastic sporting garments and offering bets to whomsoever listed, were a conspicuous feature of the scene. It was equally striking that they were not preaching in the desert and that they found plenty of patrons among the baser sort. I returned to my place in time to assist at the rather complicated operation of starting for the drive back to London. Putting in horses and getting vehicles into line seemed in the midst of the general crush and entanglement a process not to be facilitated even by the most liberal swearing on the part of those engaged in it. But little by little we came to the end of it; and as by this time a kind of mellow cheerfulness pervaded the upper atmosphere – the region of the perpendicular whip – even those interruptions most trying to patience were somehow made to minister to jollity. It was for people below not to get trampled to death or crunched between opposing wheel-hubs, but it was all for *them* to manage it. Above, the carnival of 'chaff' had set in, and it deepened as the lock of vehicles grew denser. As they were all locked together (with a comfortable padding of pedestrians at points of acutest contact), they contrived somehow to move together; so that we gradually got away and into the road. The four or five hours consumed on the road were simply an exchange of repartee, the profusely good-humoured savour of which, on the whole, was certainly striking. The chaff was not brilliant nor subtle nor especially graceful; and here and there it was quite too tipsy to be even articulate. But as an expression of that unbuttoning of the popular straight-jacket of which I spoke a while since, it had its wholesome and even innocent side. It took indeed frequently an importunate physical form; it sought emphasis in the use of pea-shooters and water-squirts. At its best, too, it was extremely low and rowdyish. But a stranger even of the most refined tastes might be glad to have a glimpse of this popular revel, for it would make him feel that he was learning something more about the English people. It would give a meaning to the old description of England as merry. It would remind him that the natives of that country are subject to some of the lighter of the human impulses, and that the decent, dusky vistas of the London residential streets – those discreet creations of which Thackeray's Baker Street is the type – are not a complete symbol of the complicated race that erected them.

II

It seemed to me such a piece of good fortune to have been asked down to Oxford at Commemoration by a gentleman implicated in the remarkable ceremony which goes on under that name, who kindly offered me the hospitality of his college, that I scarcely stayed even to thank him – I simply went and awaited him. I had had a glimpse of Oxford in former years, but I had never slept in a low-browed room looking out on a grassy quadrangle and opposite a mediaeval clock-tower. This satisfaction was vouchsafed me on the night of my arrival; I was made free of the rooms of an absent undergraduate. I sat in his deep armchairs; I burned his candles and read his books, and I hereby thank him as effusively as possible. Before going to bed I took a turn through the streets and renewed in the silent darkness that impression of the charm imparted to them by the quiet college-fronts which I had gathered in former years. The college-fronts were now quieter than ever, the streets were empty, and the old scholastic city was sleeping in the warm starlight. The undergraduates had retired in large numbers, encouraged in this impulse by the collegiate authorities, who deprecate their presence at Commemoration. However many young gownsmen may be sent away, there yet always remain a collection sufficient to represent the sound of many voices. There can be no better indication of the resources of Oxford in a spectacular way than this fact that the first step toward preparing an impressive ceremony is to get rid of as many as possible of the actors.

In the morning I breakfasted with a young American who, in common with a number of his countrymen, had come hither to seek stimulus for a finer strain of study. I know not whether he would have reckoned as such stimulus the conversation of a couple of those ingenuous youths, sons of the soil, whose society I always find charming; but it added, from my own point of view, in respect to the place, to the element of intensity of character. After the entertainment was over I repaired, in company with a crowd of ladies and elderly people, interspersed with gownsmen, to the hoary rotunda of the Sheldonian theatre, which every visitor to Oxford will remember from its curious cincture of clumsily carven heads of warriors and sages perched upon stone posts. The interior of this edifice is the scene of the classic hooting, stamping, and cat-calling by which the undergraduates confer the last consecration upon the distinguished gentlemen who come up for the honorary degree of D.C.L. It is with the design of attenuating as much as possible this volume of sound that the heads of colleges, on the close of the term, a few days before Commemoration, speed their too demonstrative disciples upon the homeward way. As I have already hinted, however, the contingent of irreverence was on this occasion quite large enough to preserve the type of the racket. This made the scene a very singular one. An American of course, with his fondness for antiquity, his relish for picturesqueness, his 'emotional' attitude at historic shrines, takes Oxford much more seriously than its sometimes unwilling familiars can be expected to do. These people are not always upon the high horse; they are not always in a state of fine vibration. Nevertheless, there is a certain maximum of disaccord with their beautiful circumstances which the ecstatic outsider vaguely expects them not to transcend. No effort of the intellect beforehand would enable him to imagine one of those silver-gray temples of learning converted into a semblance of the Bowery Theatre when the Bowery Theatre is being trifled with.

The Sheldonian edifice, like everything at Oxford, is more or less monumental. There is a double tier of galleries, with sculptured pulpits protruding from them; there are full-length portraits of kings and worthies; there is a general air of antiquity and dignity, which, on the occasion of which I speak, was enhanced by the presence of certain ancient scholars seated in crimson robes in high-backed chairs. Formerly, I believe, the undergraduates were placed apart – packed together in a corner of one of the galleries. But now they are scattered among the general spectators, a large number of whom are ladies. They muster in especial force, however, on the floor of the theatre, which has been cleared of its benches. Here the dense mass is at last severed in twain by the entrance of the prospective D.C.L.'s walking in single file, clad in crimson gowns, preceded by mace-bearers and accompanied by the Regius Professor of Civil Law, who presents them individually to the Vice-Chancellor of the University, in a Latin speech which is of course a glowing eulogy. The five gentlemen to whom this distinction had been offered in 1877 were not among those whom fame has trumpeted most loudly; but there was something 'as pretty as a picture' in their standing in their honourable robes, with heads modestly bent, while the orator, as effectively draped, recited their titles sonorously to the venerable dignitary in the high-backed chair. Each of them, when the little speech is ended, ascends the steps leading to the chair; the Vice-Chancellor bends forward and shakes his hand, and the new D.C.L. goes and sits in the blushing row of his fellow doctors. The impressiveness of all this is much diminished by the boisterous conduct of the 'students', who superabound in extravagant applause, in impertinent interrogation and in lively disparagement of the orator's Latinity. Of the scene that precedes the episode I have just described I have given no account; vivid portrayal of it it not easy. Like the return from the Derby it is a carnival of 'chaff'; and it is a singular fact that the scholastic festival should have forcibly reminded me of the great popular 'lark'. In each case it is the same race enjoying a certain definitely chartered licence; in the young votaries of a liberal education and the London rabble on the Epsom road it is the same perfect good-humour, the same muscular jocosity.

After the presentation of the doctors came a series of

those collegiate exercises which have a generic resemblance all the world over: a reading of Latin verses
and English essays, a spouting of prize poems and
Greek paraphrases. The prize poem alone was somewhat
attentively listened to; the other things were received
with an infinite variety of critical ejaculation. But after
all, I reflected as the ceremony drew to a close, the
romping element is more characteristic than it seems; it
is at bottom only another expression of the venerable
and historic side of Oxford. It is tolerated because it is
traditional; it is possible because it is classical. Looked at
in this light it became romantically continuous with the
human past that everything else referred to.

I was not obliged to find ingenious pretexts for thinking well of another ceremony of which I was witness
after we adjourned from the Sheldonian theatre. This
was a lunch-party at the particular college in which I
should find it the highest privilege to reside and which
I may not further specify. Perhaps indeed I may go so
far as to say that the reason for my dreaming of this
privilege is that it is deemed by persons of a reforming
turn the best-appointed abuse in a nest of abuses. A
commission for the expurgation of the universities has
lately been appointed by Parliament to look into it – a
commission armed with a gigantic broom, which is
to sweep away all the fine old ivied and cobwebbed
improprieties. Pending these righteous changes, one
would like while one is about it – about, that is, this
business of admiring Oxford – to attach one's self to the
abuse, to bury one's nostrils in the rose before it is
plucked. At the college in question there are no under-

graduates. I found it agreeable to reflect that those gray-green cloisters had sent no delegates to the slangy congregation I had just quitted. This delightful spot exists for the satisfaction of a small society of Fellows who, having no dreary instruction to administer, no noisy hobbledehoys to govern, no obligations but toward their own culture, no care save for learning as learning and truth as truth, are presumably the happiest and most charming people in the world. The party invited to lunch assembled first in the library of the college, a cool, gray hall, of very great length and height, with vast wall-spaces of rich-looking book-titles and statues of noble scholars set in the midst. Had the charming Fellows ever anything more disagreeable to do than to finger these precious volumes and then to stroll about together in the grassy courts, in learned comradeship, discussing their precious contents? Nothing, apparently, unless it were to give a lunch at Commemoration in the dining-hall of the college. When lunch was ready there was a very pretty procession to go to it. Learned gentlemen in crimson gowns, ladies in bright finery, paired slowly off and marched in a stately diagonal across the fine, smooth lawn of the quadrangle, in a corner of which they passed through a hospitable door. But here we cross the threshold of privacy; I remained on the further side of it during the rest of the day. But I brought back with me certain memories of which, if I were not at the end of my space, I should attempt a discreet adumbration: memories of a *fête champêtre* in the beautiful gardens of one of the other colleges – charming lawns and spreading trees, music of Grenadier Guards, ices in striped marquees, mild flirtation of youthful gownsmen and bemuslined maidens; memories, too, of quiet dinner in common-room, a decorous, excellent repast; old portraits on the walls and great windows open upon the ancient court, where the afternoon light was fading in the stillness; superior talk upon current topics, and over all the peculiar air of Oxford – the air of liberty to care for the things of the mind assured and secured by machinery which is in itself a satisfaction to sense.

In Warwickshire

There is no better way to plunge *in medias res*, for the stranger who wishes to know something of England, than to spend a fortnight in Warwickshire. It is the core and centre of the English world; midmost England, unmitigated England. The place has taught me a great many English secrets; I have been interviewing the genius of pastoral Britain. From a charming lawn – a lawn delicious to one's sentient boot-sole – I looked without obstruction at a sombre, soft, romantic mass whose outline was blurred by mantling ivy. It made a perfect picture, and in the foreground the great trees overarched their boughs, from right and left, so as to give it a majestic frame. This interesting object was the castle of Kenilworth. It was within distance of an easy walk, but one hardly thought of walking to it, any more than one would have thought of walking to a purple-shadowed tower in the background of a Berghem or a Claude. Here were purple shadows and slowly shifting lights, with a soft-hued, bosky country for the middle distance.

Of course, however, I did walk over to the castle; and of course the walk led me through leafy lanes and beside the hedgerows that make a tangled screen for large lawn-like meadows. Of course too, I am bound to add, there was a row of ancient pedlars outside the castle-wall, hawking twopenny pamphlets and photographs. Of course, equally, at the foot of the grassy mound on which the ruin stands were half a dozen public-houses and, always of course, half a dozen beery vagrants sprawling on the grass in the moist sunshine. There was the usual respectable young woman to open the castle-gate and to receive the usual sixpenny fee. There were the usual squares of printed cardboard, suspended upon venerable surfaces, with further enumeration of twopence, three-pence, fourpence. I do not allude to these things queru-lously, for Kenilworth is a very tame lion – a lion that, in former years, I had stroked more than once. I remember perfectly my first visit to this romantic spot; how I chanced upon a picnic; how I stumbled over beer-bottles; how the very echoes of the beautiful ruin seemed to have dropped all their *h*'s. That was a sultry afternoon; I allowed my spirits to sink and I came away hanging my head. This was a beautiful fresh morning, and in the interval I had grown philosophic. I had learned that, with regard to most romantic sites in England, there is a constant cockneyfication with which you must make your account. There are always people on the field before you, and there is generally something being drunk on the premises.

I hoped, on the occasion of which I am now speaking, that the attack would not be acute, and indeed for the first five minutes I flattered myself that this was the case. In the beautiful grassy court of the castle, on my entrance, there were not more than eight or ten fellow intruders. There were a couple of old ladies on a bench, eating something out of a newspaper; there was a dissenting minister, also on a bench, reading the guide-book aloud to his wife and sister-in-law; there were three or four children pushing each other up and down the turfy hillocks. This was sweet seclusion indeed; and I got a capital start with the various noble square-windowed fragments of the stately pile. They are extremely majestic, with their even, pale-red colour, their deep-green drapery, their princely vastness of scale. But presently the tranquil ruin began to swarm like a startled hive. There were plenty of people, if they chose to show themselves. They emerged from crumbling doorways and gaping chambers with the best conscience in the world; but I know not, after all, why I should bear them a grudge, for they gave me a pretext for wandering about in search of a quiet point of view. I cannot say that I found my point of view, but in looking for it I saw the castle, which is certainly an admirable ruin. And when the respectable young woman had let me out of the gate again, and I had shaken my head at the civil-spoken pedlars who form a little avenue for the arriving and departing visitor, I found it in my good-nature to linger a moment on the trodden, grassy slope, and to think that in spite of the hawkers, the paupers and the beer-shops, there was still a good deal of old England in the scene. I say in spite of these things, but it may have been, in some degree, because of them. Who shall resolve into its component parts any impression of this richly complex English world, where the present is always seen, as it were, in profile, and the past presents a full face? At all events the solid red castle rose behind me, towering above its small old ladies and its investigating parsons;

before me, across the patch of common, was a row of
ancient cottages, black-timbered, red-gabled, pictorial,
which evidently had a memory of the castle in its better
days. A quaintish village straggled away on the right, and
on the left the dark, fat meadows were lighted up with
misty sun-spots and browsing sheep. I looked about
for the village stocks; I was ready to take the modern
vagrants for Shakespearean clowns; and I was on the
point of going into one of the ale-houses to ask Mrs
Quickly for a cup of sack.

I began these remarks, however, with no intention of
talking about the celebrated curiosities in which this
region abounds, but with a design rather of noting a
few impressions of some of the shyer and more elusive
ornaments of the show. Stratford of course is a very
sacred place, but I prefer to say a word, for instance,
about a charming old rectory a good many miles distant,
and to mention the pleasant picture it made, of a summer
afternoon, during a domestic festival. These are the
happiest of a stranger's memories of English life, and he
feels that he need make no apology for lifting the corner
of the curtain. I drove through the leafy lanes I spoke of
just now, and peeped over the hedges into fields where
the yellow harvest stood waiting. In some places they
were already shorn, and, while the light began to redden
in the west and to make a horizontal glow behind
the dense wayside foliage, the gleaners here and there
came brushing through gaps in the hedges with enor-
mous sheaves upon their shoulders. The rectory was an
ancient, gabled building, of pale red brick, with facings
of white stone and creepers that wrapped it up. It dates,

I imagine from the early Hanoverian time; and as it stood there upon its cushiony lawn and among its ordered gardens, cheek to cheek with its little Norman church, it seemed to me the model of a quiet, spacious, easy English home. The cushiony lawn, as I have called it, stretched away to the edge of a brook, and afforded to a number of very amiable people an opportunity of playing lawn-tennis. There were half a dozen games going forward at once, and at each of them a great many 'nice girls', as they say in England, were distinguishing themselves. These young ladies kept the ball going with an agility worthy of the sisters and sweethearts of a race of cricketers, and gave me a chance to admire their flexibility of figure and their freedom of action. When they came back to the house, after the games, flushed a little and a little dishevelled, they might have passed for the attendant nymphs of Diana flocking in from the chase. There had, indeed, been a chance for them to wear the quiver, a target for archery being erected on the lawn. I remembered George Eliot's Gwendolen, and waited to see her step out of the muslin group; but she was not forthcoming, and it was plain that if lawn-tennis had been invented in Gwendolen's day this young lady would have captivated Mr Grandcourt by her exploits with the racket. She certainly would have been a mistress of the game; and, if the suggestion be not too gross, the alertness she would have learned from it might have proved an inducement to her boxing the ears of the insupportable Deronda.

After a while it grew too dark for lawn-tennis; but while the twilight was still mildly brilliant I wandered

away, out of the grounds of the charming parsonage, and turned into the little churchyard beside it. The
small weather-worn, rust-coloured church had an appearance of high antiquity; there were some curious Norman
windows in the apse. Unfortunately I could not get
inside; I could only glance into the open door across the
interval of an old-timbered heavy-hooded, padlocked
porch. But the sweetest evening stillness hung over
the place, and the sunset was red behind a dark row of
rook-haunted elms. The stillness seemed the greater
because three or four rustic children were playing, with
little soft cries, among the crooked, deep-buried grave-
stones. One poor little girl, who seemed deformed, had
climbed some steps that served as a pedestal for a tall,
mediaeval-looking cross. She sat perched there and
stared at me through the gloaming. This was the heart
of England, unmistakably; it might have been the very
pivot of the wheel on which her fortune revolves. One
need not be a rabid Anglican to be extremely sensible
of the charm of an English country church – and indeed
of some of the features of an English rural Sunday. In
London there is a certain flatness in the observance of
this festival; but in the country some of the ceremonies
that accompany it have an indefinable harmony with
an ancient, pastoral landscape. I made this reflection
on an occasion that is still very fresh in my memory. I
said to myself that the walk to church from a beautiful country-house, of a lovely summer afternoon, may
be the prettiest possible adventure. The house stands
perched upon a pedestal of rock and looks down from
its windows and terraces upon a shadier spot in the

wooded meadows, of which the blunted tip of a spire explains the character. A little company of people, whose costume denotes the highest pitch of civilisation, winds down through the blooming gardens, passes out of a couple of small gates and reaches the footpath in the fields. This is especially what takes the fancy of the sympathetic stranger; the level, deep-green meadows, studded here and there with a sturdy oak; the denser grassiness of the footpath, the lily-sheeted pool beside which it passes, the rustic stiles, where he stops and looks back at the great house and its wooded background. It is in the highest degree probable that he has the privilege of walking with a pretty girl, and it is morally certain that he thinks a pretty English girl the very type of the maddening magic of youth. He knows that she doesn't know how lovely is this walk of theirs; she has been taking it – or taking another quite as good – any time these twenty years. But her want of immediate intelligence only makes her the more a part of his delicate entertainment. The latter continues unbroken while they reach the little churchyard and pass up to the ancient porch, round which the rosy rustics are standing, decently and deferentially, to watch the arrival of the smarter contingent. This party takes its place in a great square pew, as large as a small room, and with seats all round, and while he listens to the respectable intonings the sympathetic stranger reads over the inscriptions on the mural tablets before him, all to the honour of the earlier bearers of a name which is, for himself, a symbol of hospitality.

When I came back to the parsonage the entertainment

had been transferred to the interior, and I had occasion to admire the maidenly vigour of all the nice girls who, after playing lawn-tennis all the afternoon, were modestly expecting to dance all the evening. And in regard to this it is not impertinent to say that from almost any group of young English creatures of this order – though preferably from such as have passed their lives in quiet country homes – an American receives a delightful impression of something that he may describe as an intimate salubrity. He notices face after face in which this rosy absence of a morbid strain – this simple, natural, affectionate development – amounts to positive beauty. If the young lady have no other beauty the air I speak of is a charm in itself; but when it is united, as it so often is, to real perfection of feature and colour the result is the most delightful thing in nature. It makes the highest type of English beauty, and to my sense there is nothing so satisfyingly high as that. Not long since I heard a clever foreigner indulge, in conversation with an English lady – a very wise and liberal woman – in a little lightly restrictive criticism of her country-women. 'It is possible,' she answered, in regard to one of his objections; 'but such as they are, they are inexpressibly dear to their husbands.' This is doubtless true of good wives all over the world; but I felt, as I listened to these words of my friend, that there is often something in an English girl-face which gives it an extra touch of *justesse*. Such as the woman is, she has here, more than elsewhere, the look of being completely and profoundly, without reservations for other uses, at the service of the man she loves. This look, after one has been a while in England, comes to seem so much a proper and indispensable part of a 'nice' face, that the absence of it appears a sign of irritability or of shallowness. Latent responsiveness to the manly appeal – that is what it means; which one must take as a very comfortable meaning.

As for the prettiness, I cannot forbear, in the face of a fresh reminiscence, to give it another word. And yet in regard to prettiness what do words avail? This was what I asked myself the other day as I looked at a young girl who stood in an old oaken parlour, the rugged panels of which made a background for her lovely head, in simple conversation with a handsome lad. I said to myself that the faces of the English young have often a perfect charm, but that this same charm is too soft and shy a thing to talk about. The face of this fair creature had a pure oval, and her clear brown eyes a quiet warmth. Her complexion was as bright as a sunbeam after rain, and she smiled in a way that made any other way of smiling than that seem a shallow grimace – a mere creaking of the facial muscles. The young man stood facing her, slowly scratching his thigh and shifting from one foot to the other. He was tall and straight, and so sun-burned that his fair hair was lighter than his complexion. He had honest, stupid blue eyes, and a simple smile that showed handsome teeth. He had the look of a gentleman. Presently I heard what they were saying. 'I suppose it's pretty big,' said the beautiful young girl. 'Yes; it's pretty big,' said the handsome young man. 'It's nicer when they are big,' said his interlocutress. The young man looked at her, and at everything in general, with his slowly apprehending blue eye, and for some time no further remark was made. 'It draws ten feet of water,' he at last went on. 'How much water is there?' said the young girl. She spoke in a charming voice. 'There are thirty feet of water,' said the young man. 'Oh, that's enough,' rejoined the damsel. I had had an idea they were flirting, and perhaps indeed that is the way it is done. It was an ancient room and extremely delightful; everything was polished over with the brownness of centuries. The chimney-piece was carved a foot thick, and the windows bore, in coloured glass, the quarterings of ancestral couples. These had stopped two hundred years before; there was nothing newer than that date. Outside the windows was a deep, broad moat, which washed the base of gray walls – gray walls spotted over with the most delicate yellow lichens.

In such a region as this mellow conservative Warwick-shire an appreciative American finds the small things quite as suggestive as the great. Everything indeed is suggestive, and impressions are constantly melting into each other and doing their work before he has had time to ask them whence they came. He can scarce go into a cottage muffled in plants, to see a genial gentle-woman and a 'nice girl', without being reminded for-sooth of 'The Small House at Allington'. Why of 'The Small House at Allington'? There is a larger house to which the ladies come up to dine; but that is surely an insufficient reason. That the ladies are charming – even that is not reason enough; for there have been other nice girls in the world than Lily Dale and other mild matrons than her mamma. Reminded, however, he is – especially when he goes out upon the lawn. Of course there is lawn-tennis, and it seems all ready for Mr Crosbie to come and take a racket. This is a small example of the way in which in the presence of English life the imagination must be constantly at play on the part of members of a race in whom it has necessarily been trained to do extra service. In driving and walking, in looking and listening, everything affected one as in some degree or other characteristic of a rich, powerful, old-fashioned society. One had no need of being told that this is a conservative county; the fact seemed written in the hedgerows and in the verdant acres behind them. Of course the owners of these things were conservative; of course they were stubbornly unwilling to see the harmonious edifice of their constituted, convenient world the least bit shaken. I had a feeling, as I went about, that I should find some very ancient and curious opinions still comfortably domiciled in the fine old houses whose clustered gables and chimneys appeared here and there, at a distance, above their ornamental woods. Imperturbable British Toryism, viewed in this vague and conjectural fashion – across the fields and behind the oaks and beeches – is by no means a thing the irresponsible stranger would wish away; it deepens the very colour of the air; it may be said to be the style of the landscape. I got a sort of constructive sense of its presence in the picturesque old towns of Coventry and Warwick, which appear to be filled with those institutions – chiefly of an eleemosynary order – that make the undoubting more undoubting still. There are ancient charities in these places – hospitals, alms-houses, asylums, infant-schools – so quaint and venerable that they almost make the existence of respectful dependence a delectable and satisfying thought. In Coventry in especial, I believe, these pious foundations are so numerous as fairly to place a premium upon personal woe. Invidious reflections apart, however, there are few things that speak more quaintly and suggestively of the old England that an American loves than these clumsy little monuments of ancient benevolence. Such an institution as Leicester's Hospital at Warwick seems indeed to exist primarily for the sake of its spectacular effect upon the American tourists, who, with the dozen rheumatic old soldiers maintained in affluence there, constitute its principal *clientèle*.

The American tourist usually comes straight to this quarter of England – chiefly for the purpose of paying his respects to the birthplace of Shakespeare. Being here, he comes to Warwick to see the castle; and being at Warwick, he comes to see the odd little theatrical-looking refuge for superannuated warriors which lurks in the shadow of one of the old gate-towers. Every one will remember Hawthorne's account of the place, which has left no touch of charming taste to be added to any reference to it. The hospital struck me as a little museum kept up for the amusement and confusion of those inquiring Occidentals who are used to seeing charity more dryly and practically administered. The old hospitallers – I am not sure, after all, whether they are necessarily soldiers, but some of them happen to be – are at once the curiosities and the keepers. They sit on benches outside of their door, at the receipt of custom, all neatly brushed and darned and ready to do you the honours.

They are only twelve in number, but their picturesque dwelling, perched upon the old city rampart and full of dusky little courts, cross-timbered gable-ends and deeply sunken lattices, seems a wonderfully elaborate piece of machinery for its humble purpose. Each of the old gentlemen must be provided with a wife or 'house-keeper'; each of them has a dusky parlour of his own; and they pass their latter days in their scoured and polished little refuge as softly and honourably as a company of retired lawgivers or pensioned soothsayers.

At Coventry I went to see a couple of old charities of a similar pattern – places with black-timbered fronts, little clean-swept courts and Elizabethan windows. One of them was a romantic residence for a handful of old women, who sat, each of them, in a cosy little bower, in a sort of mediaeval darkness; the other was a school for little boys of humble origin, and this last establishment was charming. I found the little boys playing at 'top' in a gravelled court, in front of the prettiest old building of tender-coloured stucco and painted timber, ornamented with two delicate little galleries and a fantastic porch. They were dressed in small blue tunics and odd caps, like those worn by sailors, but, if I remember rightly, with little yellow tags affixed. I was able to wander at my pleasure all over the establishment; there was no sign of pastor or master anywhere; nothing but the little yellow-headed boys playing before the ancient house and practising most correctly the Warwickshire accent. I went indoors and looked at a fine old oaken staircase; I even ascended it and walked along a gallery and peeped into a dormitory at a row of very short beds; and then

I came down and sat for five minutes on a bench hardly wider than the top rail of a fence, in a little, cold, dim refectory where there was not a crumb to be seen, nor any lingering odour of bygone repasts to be perceived. And yet I wondered how it was that the sense of many generations of boyish feeders seemed to abide there. It came, I suppose, from the very bareness and, if I may be allowed the expression, the clean-licked aspect of the place, which wore the appearance of the famous platter of Jack Sprat and his wife.

Inevitably, of course, the sentimental tourist has a great deal to say to himself about this being Shakespeare's county – about these densely grassed meadows and parks having been, to his musing eyes, the normal landscape, the green picture of the world. In Shakespeare's day, doubtless, the coat of nature was far from being so prettily trimmed as it is now; but there is one place, nevertheless, which, as he passes it in the summer twilight, the traveller does his best to believe unaltered. I allude, of course, to Charlecote Park, whose venerable verdure seems a survival from an earlier England and whose innumerable acres, stretching away, in the early evening, to vaguely seen Tudor walls, lie there like the backward years receding to the age of Elizabeth. It was, however, no part of my design in these remarks to pause before so thickly besieged a shrine as this; and if I were to allude to Stratford it would not be in connection with the fact that Shakespeare planted there, to grow for ever, the torment of his unguessed riddle. It would be rather to speak of a delightful old house, near the Avon, which struck me as the ideal home for a Shakespearean scholar, or indeed for any passionate lover of the poet. Here, with books and memories and the recurring reflection that he had taken his daily walk across the bridge at which you look from your windows straight down an avenue of fine old trees, with an ever-closed gate at the end of them and a carpet of turf stretched over the decent drive – here, I say, with old brown wainscotted chambers to live in, old polished doorsteps to lead you from one to the other, deep window-seats to sit in, with a play in your lap, here a person for whom the cares of life should have resolved themselves into a care for the greatest genius who has represented and ornamented life might find a very congruous asylum. Or, speaking a little wider of the mark, the charming, rambling, low-gabled, many-staired, much-panelled mansion would be a very agreeable home for any person of taste who should prefer an old house to a new. I find I am talking about it quite like an auctioneer; but what I chiefly had at heart was to commemorate the fact that I had lunched there and, while I lunched, kept saying to myself that there is nothing in the world so delightful as the happy accidents of old English houses.

And yet that same day, on the edge of the Avon, I found it in me to say that a new house too may be a very charming affair. But I must add that the new house I speak of had really such exceptional advantages that it could not fairly be placed in the scale. Besides, was it new after all? It must have been, and yet one's impression there was all of a kind of silvered antiquity. The place stood upon a decent Stratford road, from which it looked usual enough; but when, after sitting a while in a

charming modern drawing-room, one stepped thought-
lessly through an open window upon a verandah, one
found that the horizon of the morning call had been
wonderfully widened. I will not pretend to detail all I
saw after I stepped off the verandah; suffice it that the
spire and chancel of the beautiful old church in which
Shakespeare is buried, with the Avon sweeping its base,
were one of the elements of the vision. Then there were
the smoothest lawns in the world stretching down to
the edge of this liquid slowness and making, where the
water touched them, a line as even as the rim of a
champagne-glass – a verge near which you inevitably
lingered to see the spire and the chancel (the church was
close at hand) among the well-grouped trees, and look
for their reflection in the river. The place was a garden
of delight; it was a stage set for one of Shakespeare's
comedies – for *Twelfth Night* or *Much Ado*. Just across the
river was a level meadow, which rivalled the lawn on
which I stood, and this meadow seemed only the more
essentially a part of the scene by reason of the volumin-
ous sheep that were grazing on it. These sheep were by
no means mere edible mutton; they were poetic, historic,
romantic sheep; they were not there for their weight or
their wool, they were there for their presence and their
compositional value, and they visibly knew it. And yet,
knowing as they were, I doubt whether the wisest old
ram of the flock could have told me how to explain why
it was that this happy mixture of lawn and river and
mirrored spire and blooming garden seemed to me for
a quarter of an hour the richest corner of England.

If Warwickshire is Shakespeare's country, I found

myself not dodging the consciousness that it is also George Eliot's. The author of 'Adam Bede' and 'Middlemarch' has called the rural background of those admirable fictions by another name, but I believe it long ago ceased to be a secret that her native Warwickshire had been in her intention. The stranger who treads its eternal stretched velvet recognises at every turn the elements of George Eliot's novels – especially when he carries himself back in imagination to the Warwickshire of forty years ago. He says to himself that it would be impossible to conceive anything – anything equally rural – more sturdily central, more densely definite. It was in one of the old nestling farmhouses, beyond a hundred hedgerows, that Hetty Sorrel smiled into her milk-pans as if she were looking for a reflection of her pretty face; it was at the end of one of the leafy-pillared avenues that poor Mrs Casaubon paced up and down with her many questions. The country suggests in especial both the social and the natural scenery of 'Middlemarch'. There must be many a genially perverse old Mr Brooke there yet, and whether there are many Dorotheas or not, there must be many a well-featured and well-acred young country gentleman, of the pattern of Sir James Chettam, who, as he rides along the leafy lanes, softly cudgels his brain to know why a clever girl shouldn't wish to marry him. But I doubt whether there be many Dorotheas, and I suspect that the Sir James Chettams of the county are not often pushed to that intensity of meditation. You feel, however, that George Eliot could not have placed her heroine in a local medium better fitted to throw her fine impatience into relief – a community more likely to be startled and perplexed by a questioning attitude on the part of a well-housed and well-fed young gentlewoman.

Among the edifying days that I spent in these neighbourhoods there is one in especial of which I should like to give a detailed account. But I find on consulting my memory that the details have melted away into the single deep impression of a perfect ripeness of civilisation. It was a long excursion, by rail and by carriage, for the purpose of seeing three extremely interesting old country-houses. Our errand led us, in the first place, into Oxfordshire, through the ancient market-town of Banbury, where of course we made a point of looking out for the Cross referred to in the famous nursery-rhyme. It stood there in the most natural manner – though I am afraid it has been 'done up' – with various antique gables around it, from one of whose exiguous windows the young person appealed to in the rhyme may have looked at the old woman as she rode and heard the music of her bells. The houses we went to see have not a national reputation; they are simply interwoven figures in the rich pattern of the Midlands. They have indeed a local renown but they are not thought of as unexampled, still less as abnormal, and the stranger has a feeling that his surprises and ecstasies are held to betray the existence, on his part, of a blank background. Such places, to a Warwickshire mind of good habits, must appear the pillars and props of a heaven-appointed order of things; and accordingly, in a land on which heaven smiles, they are as natural as the geology of the county or the supply of mutton. But nothing could well give a stranger a stronger impression of the wealth of England in such matters – of the interminable list of her territorial homes – than this fact that the so eminent specimens I speak of should have but a limited fame, should not be lions of the first magnitude. Of one of them, the finest in the group, one of my companions, who lived but twenty miles away, had never even heard. Such a place was not thought a subject for local swagger. Its peers and mates are scattered all over the country; half of them are not even mentioned in the county guide-books. You stumble upon them in a drive or a walk. You catch a glimpse of an ivied front at some midmost point of wide acres, and taking your way, by leave of a serious old woman at a lodge-gate, along an overarching avenue, you find yourself introduced to an edifice so human-looking in its beauty that it seems for the occasion fairly to reconcile art and morality.

To Broughton Castle, the first seen in this beautiful group, I must do no more than allude; but this is not because I failed to think it, as I think every house I see, the most delightful habitation in England. It lies rather low, and its woods and pastures slope down to it; it has a deep, clear moat all round it, spanned by a bridge that passes under a charming old gate-tower, and nothing can be sweeter than to see its clustered walls of yellow-brown stone so sharply islanded while its gardens bloom on the other side of the water. Like several other houses in this part of the country, Broughton Castle played a part (on the Parliamentary side) in the civil wars, and not the least interesting features of its beautiful interior are the several mementoes of Cromwell's station there. It was within a moderate drive of this place that in 1642 the battle of Edgehill was fought – the first great battle of the war – and gained by neither party. We went to see the battlefield, where an ancient tower and an artificial ruin (of all things in the world) have been erected for the entertainment of convivial visitors. These ornaments are perched upon the edge of a slope which commands a view of the exact scene of the contest, upwards of a mile away. I looked in the direction indicated and saw misty meadows a little greener perhaps than usual and colonnades of elms a trifle denser. After this we paid our respects to another old house which is full of memories and suggestions of that most dramatic period of English history. But of Compton Wyniates (the name of this seat of enchantment) I despair of giving any coherent or adequate account. It belongs to the Marquis of Northampton, and it stands empty all the year round. It sits on the grass at the bottom of a wooden hollow, and the glades of a superb old park go wandering upward away from it. When I came out in front of the house from a short and steep but stately avenue I said to myself that here surely we had arrived at the farthest limits of what ivy-smothered brick-work and weather-beaten gables, conscious old windows and clustered mossy roofs can accomplish for the eye. It is impossible to imagine a more finished picture. And its air of solitude and delicate decay – of having been dropped into its grassy hollow as an ancient jewel is deposited upon a cushion, and being shut in from the world and back into the past by its circling woods – all this drives the impression well home. The house is not large, as great houses go, and it sits, as

I have said, upon the grass, without even a flagging or a footpath to conduct you from the point where the avenue stops to the beautiful sculptured doorway which admits you into the small, quaint inner court. From this court you are at liberty to pass through the crookedest series of oaken halls and chambers, adorned with treasures of old wainscotting and elaborate doors and chimney-pieces. Outside, you may walk all round the house on a grassy bank, which is raised above the level on which it stands, and find it from every point of view a more charming composition. I should not omit to mention that Compton Wyniates is supposed to have been in Scott's eye when he described the dwelling of the old royalist knight in 'Woodstock'. In this case he simply transferred the house to the other side of the county. He has indeed given several of the features of the place, but he has not given what one may call its colour. I must add that if Sir Walter could not give the colour of Compton Wyniates, it is useless for any other writer to try. It is a matter for the brush and not for the pen.

And what shall I say of the colour of Wroxton Abbey, which we visited last in order and which in the thickening twilight, as we approached its great ivy-muffled face, laid on the mind the burden of its felicity? Wroxton Abbey, as it stands, is a house of about the same period as Compton Wyniates – the latter years, I suppose, of the sixteenth century. But it is quite another affair. The place is inhabited, 'kept up', full of the most interesting and most splendid detail. Its happy occupants, however, were fortunately not in the act of staying there (happy occupants, in England, are almost always absent), and the house was exhibited with a civility worthy of its merit. Everything that in the material line can render life noble and charming has been gathered into it with a profusion which makes the whole place a monument to past opportunity. As I wandered from one rich room to another and looked at these things that intimate appeal to the romantic sense which I just mentioned was mercilessly emphasised. But who can tell the story of the romantic sense when that adventurer really rises to the occasion – takes its ease in an old English country-house while the twilight darkens the corners of expressive rooms and the victim of the scene, pausing at the window, turns his glance from the observing portrait of a handsome ancestral face and sees the great soft billows of the lawn melt away into the park?

Abbeys and Castles

It is a frequent perception with the stranger in England that the beauty and interest of the country are private property and that to get access to them a key is always needed. The key may be large or it may be small, but it must be something that will turn a lock. Of the things that contribute to the happiness of an American observer in these tantalising conditions, I can think of very few that do not come under this definition of private property. When I have mentioned the hedgerows and the churches I have almost exhausted the list. You can enjoy a hedgerow from the public road, and I suppose that even if you are a Dissenter you may enjoy a Norman abbey from the street. If therefore you talk of anything beautiful in England, the presumption will be that it is private; and indeed such is my admiration of this delightful country that I feel inclined to say that if you talk of anything private the presumption will be that it is beautiful. This is something of a dilemma. When the observer permits himself to commemorate charming impressions he is in danger of giving to the world the fruits of friendship and hospitality. When on the other hand he withholds his impression he lets something admirable slip away without having marked its passage, without having done it proper honour. He ends by mingling discretion with enthusiasm, and he says to himself that it is not treating a country ill to talk of its treasures when the mention of each has tacit reference to some kindness conferred.

The impressions I have in mind in writing these lines were gathered in a part of England of which I had not before had even a traveller's glimpse; but as to which, after a day or two, I found myself quite ready to agree with a friend who lived there and who knew and loved it well, when he said very frankly 'I do believe it is the loveliest corner of the world!' This was not a dictum to quarrel about, and while I was in the neighbourhood I was quite of his opinion. I felt I might easily come to care for it very much as he cared for it; I had a glimpse of the kind of romantic passion such a country may inspire. It is a capital example of that density of feature which is the great characteristic of English scenery. There are no waste details; everything in the landscape is something particular – has a history, has played a part, has a value to the imagination. It is a region of hills and blue undulations, and, though none of the hills are high, all of them are interesting – interesting as such things are interesting in an old, small country, by a kind of exquisite modulation, something suggesting that outline and colouring have been retouched and refined by the hand of time. Independently of its castles and abbeys, the definite relics of the ages, such a landscape seems charged and interfused. It has, has always had, human relations and is intimately conscious of them. That little speech about the loveliness of his county, or of his own part of his county, was made to me by my companion as we walked up the grassy slope of a hill, or 'edge', as it is called there, from the crest of which we seemed in an instant to look away over most of the remainder of England. Certainly one would have grown to love such a view as that quite in the same way as to love some magnificent yet sensitive friend. The 'edge' plunged down suddenly, as if the corresponding slope on the other side had been excavated, and you might follow the long ridge for the space of an afternoon's walk with this vast, charming prospect before your eyes. Looking across an English county into the next but one is a very pretty entertainment, the county seeming by no means so small as might be supposed. How can a county seem small in which, from such a vantage-point as the one I speak of, you see, as a darker patch across the lighter green, the great territory of one of the greatest representatives of territorial greatness? These things constitute immensities, and beyond them are blue undulations of varying tone, and then another bosky province which furnishes forth, as you are told, the residential and other umbrage of another magnate. And to right and left of these, in wooded expanses, lie other domains of equal consequence. It was therefore not the smallness but the vastness of the country that struck me, and I was not at all in the mood of a certain American who once, in my hearing, burst out laughing at an English answer to my inquiry as to whether my interlocutor often saw Mr B —. 'Oh no,' the answer had been, 'we never see him: he lives away off in the West.' It was the western part of his county our friend meant, and my American humorist found matter for infinite jest in his meaning. 'I should as soon think,' he remarked, 'of talking of my own west or east foot.'

I do not think, even, that my sensibility to the charm of this delightful region – for its hillside prospect of old red farmhouses lighting up the dark-green bottoms of gables, and chimney-tops of great houses peeping above miles of woodland, and, in the vague places of the horizon, of far away towns and sites that one had always heard of – was conditioned upon having 'property' in the neighbourhood, so that the little girls in the town should suddenly drop curtsies to me in the street; though that too would certainly have been pleasant. At the same time having a little property would without doubt have made the attachment stronger. People who wander about the world without money in their pockets indulge in dreams – dreams of the things they would buy if their pockets were workable. These dreams are very apt to have relation to a good estate in any neighbourhood in which the wanderer may happen to find himself. For myself, I have never been in a country so unattractive that I didn't find myself 'drawn' to its most exemplary mansion. In New England and other portions of the United States I have felt my heart go out to the Greek temple, the small Parthenon, in white-painted wood; in Italy I have made imaginary proposals for the yellow-walled villa with statues on the roof. My fancy, in England, has seldom fluttered so high as the very best house, but it has again and again hovered about one of the quiet places, unknown to fame, which are locally spoken of as merely 'good'. There was one in especial, in the neighbourhood I allude to, as to which the dream of having impossibly acquired it from an embarrassed owner kept melting into the vision of 'moving in' on the morrow. I saw this place unfortunately, to small advantage; I saw it in the rain, but I am glad fine weather didn't meddle with the affair, for the irritation of envy might in this case have poisoned the impression. It was a long, wet Sunday, and the waters were deep. I had been in the house all day, for the weather can best be described by my saying that it had been deemed to exonerate us from church. But in the afternoon, the prospective interval between lunch and tea assuming formidable proportions, my host took me a walk, and in the course of our walk he led me into a park which he described as 'the paradise of a small English country-gentleman'. It was indeed a modern Eden, and the trees might have been trees of knowledge. They were of high antiquity and magnificent girth and stature; they were strewn over the grassy levels in extraordinary profusion, and scattered upon and down the slopes in a fashion than which I have seen nothing more felicitous since I last looked at the chestnuts above the Lake of Como. The point was that the property was small, but that one could perceive nowhere any limit. Shortly before we turned into the park the rain had renewed itself, so that we were awkwardly wet and muddy; but, being near the house, my companion proposed to leave his card in a neighbourly way. The house was most agreeable: it stood on a kind of terrace, in the middle of a lawn and garden, and the terrace overhung one of the most copious rivers in England, as well as looking across to those blue undulations of which I have already spoken.

On the terrace also was a piece of ornamental water, and there was a small iron paling to divide the lawn from the park. All this I beheld in the rain. My companion gave his card to the butler with the remark that we were too much bespattered to come in, and we turned away to complete our circuit. As we turned away I became acutely conscious of what I should have been tempted to call the cruelty of this proceeding. My imagination gauged the whole position. It was a blank, a blighted Sunday afternoon – no one could come. The house was charming, the terrace delightful, the oaks magnificent, the view most interesting. But the whole thing confessed to the blankness if not to the dulness. In the house was a drawing-room, and in the drawing-room was – by which I meant *must be* – an English lady, a perfectly harmonious figure. There was nothing fatuous in believing that on this rainy Sunday afternoon it would not please her to be told that two gentlemen had walked across the country to her door only to go through the ceremony of leaving a card. Therefore, when, before we had gone many yards, I heard the butler hurrying after us, I felt how just my sentiment of the situation had been. Of course we went back, and I carried my muddy boots into the drawing-room – just the drawing-room I had imagined – where I found – I will not say just the lady I had imagined, but a lady even more in keeping. Indeed there were two ladies, one of whom was staying in the house. In whatever company you find yourself in England, you may always be sure that some one present is 'staying', and you come in due time to feel the abysses within the word. The large windows of the drawing-room I speak of looked away over the river to the blurred and blotted hills, where the rain was drizzling and drifting. It was very quiet, as I say; there was an air of large leisure. If one wanted to do anything here, there was evidently plenty of time – and indeed of every other appliance – to do it. The two ladies talked about 'town': that is what people talk about in the country. If I were disposed I might represent them as talking with a positive pathos of yearning. At all events I asked myself how it could be that one should live in this charming place and trouble one's head about what was going on in London in July. Then we had fine strong tea and bread and butter.

I returned to the habitation of my friend – for I too was guilty of 'staying' – through an old Norman portal, massively arched and quaintly sculptured, across whose hollow threshold the eye of fancy might see the ghosts of monks and the shadows of abbots pass noiselessly to and fro. This aperture admits you to a beautiful ambulatory of the thirteenth century – a long stone gallery or cloister, repeated in two stories, with the interstices of its traceries now glazed, but with its long, low, narrow, charming vista still perfect and picturesque, with its flags worn away by monkish sandals and with huge round-arched doorways opening from its inner side into great rooms roofed like cathedrals. These rooms are furnished with narrow windows, of almost defensive aspect, set in embrasures three feet deep and ornamented with little grotesque mediaeval faces. To see one of the small monkish masks grinning at you while you dress and undress, or while you look up in the intervals of inspiration from your letter-writing, is a mere detail in the entertainment of living in a *ci-devant* priory. This entertainment is inexhaustible; for every step you take in such a house confronts you in one way or another with the remote past. You devour the documentary, you inhale the historic. Adjoining the house is a beautiful ruin, part of the walls and windows and bases of the piers of the magnificent church administered by the predecessor of your host, the mitred abbot. These relics are very desultory, but they are still abundant, and they testify to the great scale and the stately beauty of the abbey. You may lie upon the grass at the base of an ivied fragment, measure the girth of the great stumps of the central columns, half smothered in soft creepers, and think how strange it is that in this quiet hollow, in the midst of lonely hills, so exquisite and elaborate a work of art should have risen. It is but an hour's walk to another great ruin, which has held together more completely. There the central tower stands erect to half its altitude and the round arches and massive pillars of the nave make a perfect vista on the unencumbered turf. You get an impression that when catholic England was in her prime great abbeys were as thick as milestones. By native amateurs even now the region is called 'wild', though to American eyes it seem almost suburban in its smoothness and finish. There is a noiseless little railway running through the valley, and there is an ancient little town at the abbey-gates – a town indeed with no great din of vehicles, but with goodly brick houses, with a dozen 'publics', with tidy, whitewashed cottages, and with little girls, as I have said, bobbing curtsies in the street. Yet even now, if one had wound one's way into the valley by the railroad, it would be rather a surprise to find a great architectural display in a setting so peaceful and pastoral. How impressive then must the beautiful church have been in the days of its prosperity, when the pilgrim came down to it from the grassy hillside and its bells made the stillness sensible! The abbey was in those days a great affair; it sprawled, as my companion said, all over the place. As you walk away from it you think you have got to the end of its geography, but you encounter it still in the shape of a rugged outhouse enriched with an early-English arch, of an ancient well hidden in a kind of sculptured cavern. It is noticeable that even if you are a traveller from a land where there are no early-English – and indeed few late-English – arches, and where the well-covers are, at their hoariest, of fresh-looking shingles, you grow used with little delay to all this antiquity. Anything very old seems extremely natural; there is nothing we suffer to get so near us as the tokens of the remote. It is not too much to say that after spending twenty-four hours in a house that is six hundred years old you seem yourself to have lived in it six hundred years. You seem yourself to have hollowed the flags with your tread and to have polished the oak with your touch. You walk along the little stone gallery where the monks used to pace, looking out of the Gothic window-places at their beautiful church, and you pause at the big, round, rugged doorway that admits you to what is now the drawing-room. The massive step by which you ascend to the threshold is a trifle crooked, as it should be; the lintels are cracked and worn by the myriad-fingered years. This strikes your casual glance. You look up and down the miniature cloister before you pass in; it seems wonderfully old and queer. Then you turn into the drawing-room, where you find modern conversation and late publications and the prospect of dinner. The new life and the old have melted together; there is no dividing-line. In the drawing-room wall is a queer funnel-shaped hole, with the broad end inward, like a small casemate. You ask what it is, but people have forgotten. It is something of the monks; it is a mere detail. After dinner you are told that there is of course a ghost – a gray friar who is seen in the dusky hours at the end of passages. Sometimes the servants see him; they afterwards go surreptitiously to sleep in the village. Then, when you take your chamber-candle and go wandering bedward by a short cut through empty rooms, you are conscious of an attitude toward the gray friar which you hardly know whether to read as a fond hope or as a great fear.

A friend of mine, an American, who knew this country, had told me not to fail, while I was in the neighbourhood, to go to Stokesay and two or three other places. 'Edward IV and Elizabeth,' he said, 'are still hanging about there.' So admonished, I made a point of going at least to Stokesay, and I saw quite what my friend meant. Edward IV and Elizabeth indeed are still to be met almost anywhere in the county; as regards domestic architecture few parts of England are still more vividly old-English. I have rarely had, for a couple of hours, the sensation of dropping back personally into the past so straight as while I lay on the grass beside the well in the little sunny court of this small castle and lazily appreciated the still definite details of mediaeval life. The place is a capital example of a small *gentilhommière* of the thirteenth century. It has a good deep moat, now filled with wild verdure, and a curious gatehouse of a much later period – the period when the defensive attitude had been well-nigh abandoned. This gatehouse, which is not in the least in the style of the habitation, but gabled and heavily timbered, with quaint cross-beams protruding from surfaces of coarse white plaster, is a very effective anomaly in regard to the little gray fortress on the other side of the court. I call this a fortress, but it is a fortress which might easily have been taken, and it must have assumed its present shape at a time when people had ceased to peer through narrow slits at possible besiegers. There are slits in the outer walls for such peering, but they are noticeably broad and not particularly oblique, and might easily have been applied to the uses of a peaceful parley. This is part of the charm of the place; human life there must have lost an earlier grimness; it was lived in by people who were beginning to believe in good intentions. They must have lived very much together; that is one of the most obvious reflections in the court of a mediaeval dwelling. The court was not always grassy and empty, as it is now, with only a couple of gentlemen in search of impressions lying at their length, one of them handling a wine-flask that colours the clear water drawn from the well into a couple of tumblers by a decent, rosy, smiling, talking old woman who has come bustling out of the gatehouse and who has a large, dropsical, innocent husband standing about on crutches in the sun and making no sign when you ask after his health. This poor man has reached that ultimate depth of human simplicity at which even a chance to talk about one's ailments is not appreciated. But the civil old woman talks for every one, even for an artist who has come out of one of the rooms, where I see him afterward reproducing its mouldering repose. The rooms are all unoccupied and in a state of extreme decay, though the castle is, as yet, far from being a ruin. From one of the windows I see a young lady sitting under a tree, across a meadow, with her knees up, dipping something into her mouth. It is indubitably a camel's hair paint-brush; the young lady is inevitably sketching. These are the only besiegers to which the place is exposed now, and they can do no great harm, as I doubt whether the young lady's aim is very good. We wandered about the empty interior, thinking it a pity such things should fall to pieces. There is a beautiful great hall – great, that is, for a small castle (it would be extremely handsome in a modern house) – with tall, ecclesiastical-looking windows and a long staircase at one end, which climbs against the wall into a spacious bedroom. You may still apprehend very well the main lines of that simpler life; and it must be said that, simpler though it was, it was apparently by no means destitute of many of our own conveniences. The chamber at the top of the staircase ascending from the hall is charming still, with its irregular shape, its low-browed ceiling, its cupboards in the walls, its deep bay window formed of a series of small lattices. You can fancy people stepping out from it upon the platform of the staircase, whose rugged wooden logs, by way of steps, and solid, deeply guttered hand-rail, still remain. They looked down into the hall, where, I take it, there was always a congregation of retainers, much lounging and waiting and passing to and fro, with a door open into the court. The court, as I said just now, was not the grassy, aesthetic spot which you may find it at present of a summer's day; there were beasts tethered in it, and hustling men at arms, and the earth was trampled into puddles. But my lord or my lady, looking down from the chamber-door, commanded the position and, no doubt, issued their orders accordingly. The sight of the groups on the floor beneath, the calling up and down, the oaken tables spread and the brazier in the middle – all this seemed present again; and it was not difficult to pursue the historic vision through the rest of the building – through the portion which connected the great hall with the tower (where the confederate of the sketching young lady without had set up the peaceful three-legged engine of his craft); through the dusky, roughly circular rooms of the tower itself, and up the corkscrew staircase of the same to that most charming part of every old castle, where visions must leap away off the battlements to elude you – the bright, dizzy platform at the tower-top, the place where the castle-standard hung and the vigilant inmates surveyed the approaches. Here, always, you really overtake the impression of the place – here, in the sunny stillness, it seems to pause, panting a little, and give itself up.

It was not only at Stokesay that I lingered a while on the summit of the keep to enjoy the complete impression so overtaken. I spent such another half-hour at Ludlow, which is a much grander and more famous monument. Ludlow, however, is a ruin – the most impressive and magnificent of ruins. The charming old town and the admirable castle form a capital object of pilgrimage. Ludlow is an excellent example of a small English provincial town that has not been soiled and disfigured by industry; it exhibits no tall chimneys and smoke-streamers, no attendant purlieus and slums. The little city is perched upon a hill near which the goodly Severn wanders, and it has a remarkable air of civic dignity. Its streets are wide and clean, empty and a little grass-grown, and bordered with spacious, mildly ornamental brick houses which look as if there had been more going on in them in the first decade of the century than there is in the present, but which can still nevertheless hold up their heads and keep their window-panes clear, their knockers brilliant and their door-steps whitened. The place seems to say that some hundred years ago it was the centre of a large provincial society and that this society was very 'good' of its kind. It must have transported itself to Ludlow for the season – in rumbling coaches and heavy curricles – and there entertained itself in decent emulation of that more majestic capital which a choice of railway lines had not as yet placed within its immediate reach. It had balls at the assembly rooms; it had Mrs Siddons to play; it had Catalani to sing. Miss Burney's and Miss Austen's heroines might perfectly well have had their first love-affair there; a journey to Ludlow would certainly have been a great event to Fanny Price or Emma Woodhouse, or even to those more romantically connected young ladies Evelina and Cecilia. It is a place on which a provincial aristocracy has left so sensible a stamp as to enable you to measure both the grand manners and the small ways. It is a very interesting array of houses of the period after the poetry of domestic architecture had begun to wane and before the vulgarity had come – a fine familiar classic prose. Such places, such houses, such relics and intimations, carry us back to the near antiquity of that pre-Victorian England which it is still easy for a stranger to picture with a certain vividness, thanks to the partial survival of many of its characteristics. It is still easier for a stranger who has dwelt a time in England to form an idea of the tone, the habits, the aspect of the social life before its classic insularity had begun to wane, as all observers agree that it did about thirty years ago. It is true that the mental operation in this matter reduces itself to our imagining some of the things which form the peculiar national notes as infinitely exaggerated: the rigidly aristocratic constitution of society, the unaesthetic temper of the people, the small public fund of convenience, of elegance. Let an old gentleman of conservative tastes, who can remember the century's youth, talk to you at a club *temporis acti* – tell you wherein it is that from his own point of view London, as a residence for a gentleman, has done nothing but fall off for the last forty years. You will listen, of course, with an air of decent sympathy, but privately you will say to yourself how difficult a place of sojourn London must have been in those days for the traveller from other countries – how little cosmopolitan, how bound, in a thousand ways, with narrowness of custom. What was true of the great city at that time was of course doubly true of the provinces; and a community of the type of Ludlow must have been a kind of focus of insular propriety. Even then, however, the irritated alien would have had the magnificent ruins of the castle to dream himself back into good humour in. They would effectually have transported him beyond all waning or waxing Philistinisms.

THE STORY OF PENGUIN CLASSICS

Before 1946 ...'Classics' are mainly the domain of academics and students, without readable editions for everyone else. This all changes when a little-known classicist, E. V. Rieu, presents Penguin founder Allen Lane with the translation of Homer's Odyssey that he has been working on and reading to his wife Nelly in his spare time.

1946 The Odyssey becomes the first Penguin Classic published, and promptly sells three million copies. Suddenly, classic books are no longer for the privileged few.

1950s Rieu, now series editor, turns to professional writers for the best modern, readable translations, including Dorothy L. Sayers's *Inferno* and Robert Graves's *The Twelve Caesars*, which revives the salacious original.

1960s 1961 sees the arrival of the Penguin Modern Classics, showcasing the best twentieth-century writers from around the world. Rieu retires in 1964, hailing the Penguin Classics list as 'the greatest educative force of the 20th century'.

1970s A new generation of translators arrives to swell the Penguin Classics ranks, and the list grows to encompass more philosophy, religion, science, history and politics.

1980s The Penguin American Library joins the Classics stable, with titles such as *The Last of the Mohicans* safeguarded. Penguin Classics now offers the most comprehensive library of world literature available.

1990s Penguin Popular Classics are launched, offering readers budget editions of the greatest works of literature. Penguin Audiobooks brings the classics to a listening audience for the first time, and in 1999 the launch of the Penguin Classics website takes them online to an ever larger global readership.

The 21st Century Penguin Classics are rejacketed for the first time in nearly twenty years. This world famous series now consists of more than 1,300 titles, making the widest range of the best books ever written available to millions – and constantly redefining the meaning of what makes a 'classic'.

The Odyssey continues ...

The best books ever written

PENGUIN 🐧 CLASSICS

SINCE 1946